Create a Family Museum
and
Save Your History

HOW TO FIND SPACE, CREATE, ORGANIZE,
PRESERVE AND DISPLAY FAMILY HEIRLOOMS,
TREASURES AND MEMORIES

Written by
Elizabeth Goesel
Family Museum Curator

HERITAGE BOOKS
2017

HERITAGE BOOKS

AN IMPRINT OF HERITAGE BOOKS, INC.

Books, CDs, and more—Worldwide

For our listing of thousands of titles see our website
at
www.HeritageBooks.com

Published 2017 by
HERITAGE BOOKS, INC.
Publishing Division
5810 Ruatan Street
Berwyn Heights, Md. 20740

International Standard Book Number
Paperbound: 978-0-7884-5764-7

Table of Contents

*"It has been said that at its best,
preservation engages the past
in a conversation with the present
over a mutual concern for the future."*

~ William Murtagh,
First Keeper of the National Register of Historic Places

What Is a Family Museum?

Definition of a museum: a large building filled with galleries displaying everything from art works to Zenith TVs. Though they are magnificent institutions, they are impersonal. Displays are measured carefully; their objective is to inform and educate with cool detachment. You would love to get a closer look, even cherish the idea of touching the artifact. But this is not allowed and for good reason . . . it is not yours to do so. The artifacts and antiquities are presented in succession leading from the past to the present for future perpetuity and for all human-kind.

Definition of a family museum: a place(s) in your home (or place of work) where objects of interest or significance are exhibited, preserved and at any time can be visited, looked at and touched. Your heirlooms, keepsakes and awards offer the continuation of your family (or business) events, from days-gone-by to present-day events, to uphold and protect your family's future.

Everyone has objects of interest. Some more than others but that is subjective. Regardless of what they are, these objects are important to you, to your family, to the family's next generation; these objects need to be preserved and put on display for everyone to see, enjoy and respect.

A *Family Museum* may be hard to visualize because the space in a museum cannot be compared with the space you have. To get a good picture, visit small museums that focus on a specific era in history or personal collections of an eminent person.

Antique stores are great places to visualize the concept of display. The proprietors take pride in how they present collections to encourage you to take a closer look and possibly purchase the item. Smaller places offer an intimate viewing experience, giving you a closer look and perhaps ideas.

Your Family Museum will showcase, define, edify and entertain those who gaze upon the lovingly displayed pieces, becoming acquainted with your family's history. "Welcome, one and all. It is my pleasure to introduce you to my family . . . "

"For what is the present after all but the growth out of the past?"   ~ *Walt Whitman*

As I was creating this book, it occurred to me that the wisdom   herein focuses on an age demographic that has saved their family heirlooms over possibly generations only to find much to their dismay that their children and grandchildren do not want what was saved.

Then I ran across a quote by Richard G. Scott that hits this dilemma right on its head: *"Do you young people want a sure way to eliminate the influence of the adversary in your life? Immerse yourself in searching for your ancestors."*

These two baby toys started our Family Museum

What in essence these words impart is that it is never too late for young people to stop ignoring and throwing their history away. As this book advocates, it is just as important to save ancestral   history in way of family trees, censes records, genealogy studies, diaries, bibles, photographs, etc., but it is also about the physical property, the stuff that is in those boxes, stored away and forgotten. That is why it is so important to create a Family Museum.

If you don't know where to start, start with yourself. If you don't know what records to get and how to find them, start with what you have. This is one sure way of establishing the museum and watch the rest of the family get involved because they, too, have memories they should save.

"Creating something beautiful is compelling and addictive. It's meditation of sorts. The assemblage process, adding that you don't need anything except your eye and your chosen objects. Even if nothing else in your room pleases you, you can transform one surface to your own satisfaction. The resulting still life is like a museum of you. It's more personal, more likely to trigger funny anecdotes and less bogus than a single mass-produced aged brass bowl or vintage hourglass cranked out by Restoration Hardware. There's a longing for individuality out there."

~ Hilary Robinson

Introduction

STOP throwing or giving your Memories away
and
START creating *Your Family Museum* today

This book will not instruct you on how to unclutter your home or how to right-size, downsize, rearrange or reprioritize your life. It is about selecting, displaying and honoring your family's history by creating a special place in the home for your keepsakes, heirlooms and other artifacts that celebrate your family's heritage, giving it new meaning and value today, tomorrow and for generations to come.

We know most things these days are mass-produced, used, expended and discarded. However, what about those things that have lasted, perhaps several lifetimes? These things should be saved and passed on. If we do not preserve them, what will we have that shows proof of their existence, establishes a regard for that keepsake and builds a foundation for our family members in the future? You may agree with wanting to save your heritage, however, you don't because you think perhaps you do not have the space in your home to showcase your history. This book will explain how and where you can save your *material genealogy.* ™

I created this phrase as I constructed our *Family Museum*. Just like the study of genealogy, as you research your family's roots, you dig through all kinds of documents: courthouse papers, church records, libraries, historical sites, bibles, diaries, family trees and charts, and of course, boxes, where much unforgotten histories are stashed, bundled and tied up with string, photo albums, scrapbooks, even cookbooks, all of which are one-dimensional. Now imagine, you find a pair of baby shoes and the photograph of the person wearing them and put them together. This is *material genealogy*. Or for instance, a hairbrush that still retains wisps of hair. Can you imagine the DNA that can be discovered here? Now envision a place in your home where these precious things can be displayed and preserved, presenting many opportunities to share your family history. Instead of turning a page, scanning a family tree, reading endless works on paper, you can hold the fragile china teacup, feel the arduous weight of an iron skillet, catch a scent of baby powder on a baby blanket, slip the ring your grandmother wore on your finger, play with an old toy, wind up an old clock or music box hearing what your ancestor listened to. Touch, smell, feel, sound; all of these ignite your senses and put you in physical touch with your family history. Your *Material Genealogy*.

The book's Table of Contents headings focus on the topic of the chapter and many include personal narratives on the objects that relate to the subject matter which were selected posts from my blog, *How to Create a Family Museum.* The aim is to show and tell you why the artifact is in the museum. Perhaps the story will offer inspirations and give you some idea as to what can be saved and displayed and how to showcase it.

Enhancing the contents are several thoughtful comments that offer feedback on the topics, enlightening the importance of why a *Family Museum* should be created, which is to sustain the value of your material genealogy. Family treasures, keepsakes, mementos, antiques and collections teach us who we are and where we come from. Your Family Museum not only is a look back, it is about looking to the future. As you create your museum, you will find the endeavor edifying, entertaining and most of all FUN!

So get ready to create Your Family Museum. Make a concerted effort to preserve your heritage. It is a vital link to your cultural, educational, artistic, inspirational and economical legacies. All of the things that literally make you who you are.

One day my dear friend Barbara accompanied me to my attic. As I rearranged once again stacks of boxes to make room for more, she laughed when she spotted a box labeled *Charlie's memorabilia.*

She asked, "How could Charlie already have a box of stuff when he is only two years old?" Laughing, I said, "Open it!"

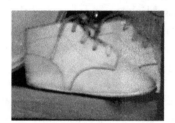

She did and was surprised to see that I had not only the usual baby shoes, she saw his teething ring, a tiny box with his baby teeth in it, first tiny diaper, Christening gown, rattles and photographs. As she closed the box, I could see a melancholy expression on her face. She said softly, "I kept Christy's baby shoes but not Ryan's. I never thought to keep the things you did." Then she laughed. "And Charlie's teeth! Ryan swallowed his and I think my grandmother kept some of Christy's, but their gone now." Handing the box back to me, she asked, "What are you going to do with all this stuff?"

Feeling overwhelmed as I gazed upon the stacked boxes, I was not at all sure what to do. Then a couple of years' later, push came to shove and I had to do something about all those boxes. My father had a stroke and my mother was terrified of taking care of him herself. Soon after, our family offered to turn the attic into an apartment for my parents. But where do put all these boxes? We piled them in the hall and as we placed these cubicles of souvenirs into stacks, we looked into each box to see what was in it. Oh my goodness! Talk about memories.

Each of us was stunned to see stuff we thought long gone and were thrilled to see again. After going through the boxes we wrote on them what was inside and put them in a large linen closet that was yet to be finished. There they sat until we knew what to do with them. A concept of a Family Museum was yet to be conceived.

Then one day my daughter and I took a trip offered by the Chrysler Museum in Norfolk, VA to the Reynolda House Museum of American Art in Winston-Salem, North Carolina. Built in 1917 by Katherine Smith Reynolds and her husband R.J. Reynolds, founder of the Reynolds Tobacco Company, the home displayed a premier collection of American art ranging from the colonial period to present.

Reynolda displays many of the furnishings selected by Katharine to decorate her home in the height of fashion for early twentieth-century America. Finely situated among the furnishings are works of art by notable artists spanning three centuries, including

Albert Bierstadt, Frederic Church, Jacob Lawrence and Grant Wood. Traveling exhibits for two shows are featured every year, one in the fall and one in the spring.

Throughout the house there are exhibits in many other rooms, but the one exhibit that caught our eyes was the one in the attic. Down the middle of this large space was a hallway lined with glassed-in mini-rooms displaying three generations of the family's clothing and accessories and a collection of children and grandchildren's toys. In Katherine Reynolds's time, the attic was where she stored her clothes, an irresistible lure to her daughters, nieces, and their friends.

After viewing these little rooms, we now had the idea of how we were going create our own Family Museum. But where was still the question. If the Reynold's family can take areas of their home to display their precious memorabilia, then so could our family. We couldn't wait to get back home and go to work!

Since my husband just finished building our home two years prior, some areas were still a work-in-progress, particularly the front hall. We did not know what style staircase we wanted, so none was built as there were stairs in the kitchen. (And their great for hanging holiday lights on!)

With the hall having no stairs, the elevator was installed. It was large enough to accommodate my father's wheelchair and another passenger. It is quite convenient to have an elevator in the house since there are four floors.

After the elevator was installed, my husband started to build the stairway, one step at a time, from the first floor to the second floor to the third floor. The space was tight but he is a skilled craftsman capable of building a magnificent staircase.

When the attic was finished, it became a private apartment with two bedrooms, bathroom, kitchen, living & dining room. Very commodious and with the ease of the elevator, my dad was able to ride it down to the basement where we had set up a workshop filled with his tools and gadgets so he could stay busy and give mom a rest. They lived there for several years until they both passed away.

Though we wanted to get started right away on building the family museum, construction was going on and the boxes sat in the closet.

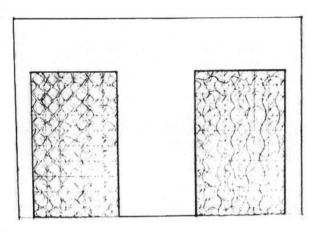

As I sat at my desk and stared out into the hall, I looked at the lacy white curtains concealing the two wide openings to the linen closet that did not have one iota of linen; it was filled with the boxes. The closet was big; 14' x 4' deep and 9' high. No doors, no shelves, and a small sliding door in the ceiling that opened up into the attic. I made up my mind that this closet was going to become our Family Museum.

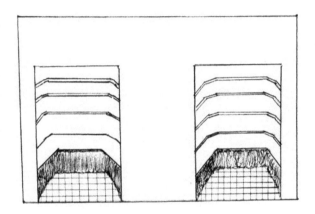

Taking out graph paper, pencil and ruler, I drew the idea of how I wanted the museum to look. Having two doors, I divided the closet into two spaces for two museums; one for my husband and I and one for our two adult children. I gave my husband the drawings and when he had the time, he built the shelves. The walls were still a builder's white, so I painted them a dark mauve. The shelves were painted yellow and I made curtains to conceal the storage space below. The floor had beige linoleum that was doable. Lighting had already been installed and the trap door sealed.

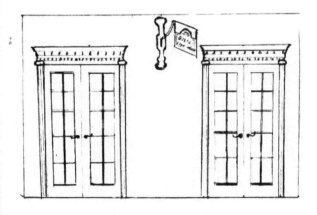

French doors were hung and framed out with handmade trim. Then a double-sided sign; our side purple, the kid's side green, announcing the Goesel Family Museum, and it is always opened.

Why a Family Should Have a Museum

You save things. You put them away. You store them thinking perhaps maybe one day it will get used again. However, that day does not come and the things are still in the box. What do you do? Throw them away? NO! Give them away? NO! What you should do is take the things out of the box, give them a fair assessment and then ask yourself if you should keep them. The answer is YES! Why? Because something possessed you to keep them in the first place.

People ask me why I have a Family Museum. Well, why not. If celebrities, sports stars, famous authors, military heroes and others can, then so can I. And so can you.

You may have vintage clothing, rare baseball cards, first edition books, Purple Hearts, antiquities. Why did you keep these things? Where are they right now? Any idea what you will do with them? YES, YOU DO! You are going to put them in your Family Museum to preserve and protect your family history.

Todays families are on the go 24/7. Time passes quickly. Age is inevitable. Memories dull. Sometimes they can even get in the way of moving on. Still, you should not forget all the important and not so important events that shaped your life. A Family Museum will help you take notice of your history and establish meaning for generations to come.

"The Heart hath its own memory, like the mind, and in it are enshrined the precious keepsakes, into which is wrought the giver's loving thought."
~ Henry Wadsworth Longfellow

Tiffeni's and Charlie's Christening Kegs

Charlie's Baby Memorabilia

Boxes in the attic. Boxes in the basement. Boxes in the garage, in the shed, and under the bed. Boxes with hastily scribbled writing on it that says baby clothes. Another says, Grandmas' bric-a-brac. The boxes from the attic may be filled with old toys, games and comic books. You know what is in the boxes stored in garage – tools! Like my father, he had dozens of coffee cans filled with oily nuts and bolts and gizmos I hadn't the slightest idea to what they were, but apparently they were important enough to him to keep. The boxes from the basement smell moldy and you are not sure if you even want to open them. But you do and much to your delight, you find your high school yearbooks. You sit down on the steps and slowly turn the stiff pages and gaze down at the faces you knew and wonder where they are now?

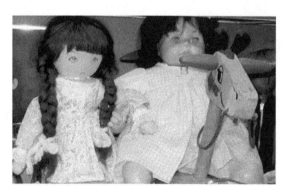

Tiffeni's Dolls and Giraffe

Keith's doll/clothes made by his mother

Keith's truck his father made

Charlies Bowling Trophies

Keith's Naval Memorabilia

Whose Things Belong in the Family Museum?

Look at it this way. If you do not display at least a few things from each member of the family, you may end up with a family feud. Sometimes this situation can be touchy especially if the family has gone through a critical time; separation, divorce, death, or a weather or fire catastrophe that wiped out many of your precious heirlooms. We all at some time in our lives experience unfortunate events. If a picture or something makes you relieve past hurt or insurmountable sadness, then don't put it in. Instead of making that decision yourself, consult the family.

So put in the prize possessions, hang up the baby shoes, and display the toys and yearbooks. Everyone's things belong in the Family Museum – a living tapestry of your family's history.

Keith's Baby Shoes

Our High School Yearbooks

Lizzie's Baby Dish

"A morsel of genuine history, a thing so rare as to be always valuable."

~ Thomas Jefferson, Third President of the United States

Whose Things Belong in the Family Museum
How about the Family Pets?

Sophie, Slippers, Jazz, Sidney, Christmas, Thumper and more. How many family pet have come into your life, stayed as long as they could, gave you unconditional love and support, and had them eating right out of your hand? How many did you rescue, purchase from a pet store, or found in your yard? Did you save anything from these lovable characters? Where are their few possessions now?

Like our family, I am sure you have many stories to tell and what better way to do so is by displaying something of theirs in your Family Museum. If you still have perhaps a toy or their bowl, include it among your heirlooms with a photograph showing them with or without the keepsakes. Your pets need to be cherished when they are with you and when they have passed on. Even while writing this little memoir, I get tears in my eyes recalling all of the great, even those not-so-fun times with my pets. Here are a few pictures of our pets and their things in our Family Museum.

Sophie Peach! What a great name and dog. She was an Old English Sheep dog, bred from a breeder of many champion sheepdogs. When we first saw her, she was on the porch in a pen playing with her brothers and sisters. Her breeder thought her to be one of the smallest in the litter and not quite worthy enough to be a show dog. Boy, was she wrong! At her young adult age, Sophie weighed over a hundred pounds and was as tall as a sofa seat. She had long legs and curly black & white fur. It always amazed us that when her fur hung over her eyes, she could still see. Then we figured out why – her eyes lashed were long and kept her fur from falling in her eyes.

Sophie had many toys, some squeaked and others made strange noises. And every one of them was called "Baby!" Eventually, her toys were in many places, so Keith built her a toy box with her name on it, and in no time at all, she learned to put her toys in the box and of course, take them out. We had lots of fun burying dog biscuits in the box and she would tip the heavy box over in search of the biscuits, and of course, we had to pick up the toys and put them back into the box. But all in fun! Pictured here is Sophie with her nightly bowl of milk and cookie before she went to sleep. And with all our hearts, we hope she is enjoying many more bowls of milk and cookies forever more.

Slippers! Here was a cat who outlived her nine lives. She was the feistiest cat I had ever known, and I have known many.

When I was 10 years old, I brought home my first kitten. Her name was Puttykins. She was very productive during her life, presenting our family with numerous litters, providing a plethora of kittens. At one time I had dozens of cats, all of which lived out in the farmland, keeping the mouse and other critter population down. One kitten what was kept was my beloved Spookie, black as midnight and my soulmate. After I was married and moved away, Spookie passed away. It was a sad day. It took a couple of years before I had another, and this one was a piece of work.

Her name was Christmas, a mixed Siamese with the bluest eyes and a vocal range that could make you cover your ears. She was with our family for 10 years and to this day, fondly remembered.

Christmas had a strange bowl she ate out of. I can't remember where I found it, but it was quirky, like her. After Christmas passed way, we adopted Slippers. But in between was another cat name Casper. He was purchased from a

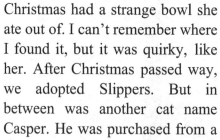

pet store and not the nicest cat I had. He was a white Angora and shed all over the place. Because he was a beautiful cat, he was stolen and though I was sad, the rest of the family was somewhat relieved, especially my husband who sneezed constantly.

We adopted Slippers from the local animal shelter. They would not take her because she had a very crooked tail and six toes on each foot. Keith names her Slippers because all four paws were white as was her check. Her fur was on the longish side and we swore she was part Siamese because she talked, not as much as Christmas did, but when she had something on her mind, she told you. Before Slippers came to live with us, we had a dog named Sidney. He, too, was adopted from a shelter because he was an accidently mixed breed, part sheep dog, part Border collie. A sheepdog with a tail. We also had a rabbit named Thumper. Oddly enough, all three animals got along and entertained us every day. When we moved to Virginia from Florida, Sid and Slips came with us, but Thumper stayed back and was adopted by another family who loved rabbits. All of them ate out of the kitty bowl!

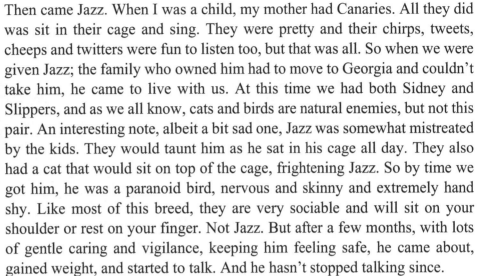

Then came Jazz. When I was a child, my mother had Canaries. All they did was sit in their cage and sing. They were pretty and their chirps, tweets, cheeps and twitters were fun to listen too, but that was all. So when we were given Jazz; the family who owned him had to move to Georgia and couldn't take him, he came to live with us. At this time we had both Sidney and Slippers, and as we all know, cats and birds are natural enemies, but not this pair. An interesting note, albeit a bit sad one, Jazz was somewhat mistreated by the kids. They would taunt him as he sat in his cage all day. They also had a cat that would sit on top of the cage, frightening Jazz. So by time we got him, he was a paranoid bird, nervous and skinny and extremely hand shy. Like most of this breed, they are very sociable and will sit on your shoulder or rest on your finger. Not Jazz. But after a few months, with lots of gentle caring and vigilance, keeping him feeling safe, he came about, gained weight, and started to talk. And he hasn't stopped talking since.

Jazz is now seventeen years old and his life expectancy gives him a few more. After recovering from his troubled past, he became friendly with Sidney and tolerated Slippers. In fact this one day when Slippers got a little to close, Jazz gave her one sharp peck on her nose, and thereafter, Slippers had a new respect for him.

As time went on, Sidney passed away and it took us several years before we brought Sophie home. Jazz liked Sophie and talked to her from high on top of his cage. When Slippers passed away, we could tell that Jazz felt her departure. But he adjusted and is now the center of our attention, bringing us much delight with his antics and loveliness.

When Jazzes departs this world, I will make a shadow box museum displaying the rings and mirror that hangs in his cage, along with his picture and a few of the many feathers he had shed through the years.

I never thought I could get close to a bird, but Jazz has taught not only me but the whole family that every family pet is just that, a member of the family, and deserves just as much loving and respect as we have for each other.

So, as you put your Family Museum together, don't forget to include the family pets. They brought you much joy when they were with you and will continue to do so when given their fair due.

Cheeps, Woofs & Meows forever more.

When Should You Start Your Family Museum?

One of the hardest things to do is to start something new. We all have the tendency to put things off. We often say, Oh, I will do it tomorrow. Or, I don't have the time now. Or, you start it and I will pitch in. Or this one; After all, tomorrow is another day.

However, once you commit yourself to this project, you may be surprised to find you are actually enjoying yourself. When you get family members involved, the project becomes a family event. Even when you think it is done, it is not. That's OK. You will find that many other things will be added, moved around, changed and you will enjoy doing it.

OK! I'll admit not everyone in the family may be as enthusiastic about the museum as you are. So instead of letting their procrastination slow you down, start with your stuff first. That is what I did and before I knew it, I could have used every shelf.

Then the husband or in some cases it can be the wife, or child or children, comes tootling by and say, Hey! What about my things? Where's my space? Oh dear! Did you have something to put in the family museum? You ask. Why, yes I/we do! Well then, let us have a look at what you want to display, and before he, she, or they know it, you got em' opening up all those boxes, pulling things out right and left, and becoming involved with creating the *Family Museum*.

As the shelves fill up, it becomes apparent how time slipped away. It will be hard to believe what seemed like 'just yesterday' is in fact, decades, maybe even a century. Time has a way of running away from us, so by preserving your heirlooms, you can take pride in those accomplishments, revisit special occasions, even recall the moments in time that changed or guided your footsteps.

"This time, like all times, is a very good one, if we but know what to do with it."
~ Ralph Waldo Emerson

From childhood to young adult, schools, careers, travels, relationships, marriage(s), parenthood and retirement, everyone moves from place to place, accumulates, inherits and buys stuff. Many boxes are filled up, moved around, some get lost, some get trashed, and some are kept. Within all of this boxed and bagged stuff, there are some worthy keepsakes. Maybe you have some of grandma's lace doilies or a china teacup. Could be that you still have your baby blanket, or your mother's wedding ring. Perhaps you have your uncle's bugle. These may be strange things, but I can assure you there are stranger things then these.

For example, when I placed my father's coal-stained paycheck stubs in the album I made for him chronicling his life, coal residue came off my fingers.

When I picked up nana's iron skillet the weight alone made me ponder how she maneuvered this heavy pan.

When my husband takes the toy truck his father made for him off the shelf to show someone, he feels his father's pride.

My father's coal

My Nana's iron skillet

Some items make you ponder; others make you laugh. Some can make you cry. And this is all well and fine because these feelings help you see and understand your ancestors, their trials and tribulations, just like yours.

As an amateur historian, I appreciate the efforts of conservators, archeologists, even treasure hunters. Yet when you go to museums to see coveted antiques, rare artifacts and treasures from the bottom of the sea, you can't help feeling disconnected. Glass walls retain you, museum guards prohibit you, and people standing in front of you diminish your ability to appreciate what you want to see.

One Generation of Time

However, when you arrange and display your heirlooms in your museum, you can touch the delicate lace on the doily, imagine the taste of the sweet tea in grandmas' china teacup, sniff the sweet smell of powder in the baby blanket, and see how your mother's wedding ring looks on your finger. Perhaps you even have your uncle's bugle. Give it a blow. Hear the shrill sound. All of your senses; sight, hearing, taste, smell, touch . . . come alive and so do the lives of those family members who sewed that lace, made the tea, bathed the baby, said I do, and didn't want to get up in the morning!

What is important is to know that as you display your family memorabilia, you are preserving your family's history. Keepsakes reveal the stages of life: baby shoes, dolls & kitchen sets, cowboys & cars, school graduations, and the top of the wedding cake. They are like those little crumbs you leave along the way as you travel down the paths you have taken through life. The things we preserve today will pass onto our children tomorrow, reestablishing our past, confirming their present, and guaranteeing that we will not be forgotten in the future.

From one generation to the next, family history gets lost. Many things go missing, leaving us with regret. So now is the time, today not tomorrow, to start creating your Family Museum. It doesn't matter what you put on the shelf. It doesn't matter if it is a replacement if the original is gone. It doesn't matter if it appears to be a piece of junk or an antiquity. It doesn't matter if it has a hole in it or it is broken. What matters is that whatever it is, it has a memory that needs to be remembered, it has a value that needs to be protected, and it has a life story that needs to be told. And not only do these things showcase you and your family's life, it represents America's and many other countries and cultures, too. Creating a Family Museum is a rich and rewarding project that will enhance your life.

"The difference between a piece of junk and an heirloom or antique is simple: one generation of time. If items can survive the junk stage for one full generation, they will become curiosities and then valuable family keepsakes and heirlooms."

(From *The Everything Family Tree Book* by ~ William G. Hartley)

My 28 year-old son, Charlie, decided to finally clean out his closet. What an undertaking he found it to be. File folders of newspaper clippings, bags of bags from places he shopped, paper tubes filled with drawings, and boxes filled with his insatiable desire to collect maritime history artifacts. He was overwhelmed with his collections and perplexed as to how he was going to sort through it all, what to keep, what to throw away and then how and where to keep his stuff. After a few hours, he came to me with eyes like a deer caught in the headlights, stunned and at a loss at what to do next. However, he does have some knowledge on how to keep what is most important to him because he has his own museum, albeit the fact that it was created for him by me, the *family museum curator*. But what he has in his possession that is not in the museum is what he needs to be concerned about. So here are a few of the suggestions and steps I encouraged him to follow:

1. Tackle one project at a time, such as going through the file folders of newspaper clippings. Review each one, measure its relevance. Separate piles in subject-like matter. Take each clipping and trim away irrelevant print, but make sure to keep the date and publication info. Repair any rips with preservation double coated tape. Either re-file kept clippings chronologically or place a few notable ones in a scrapbook designed for keeping newspaper. For a wide selection of albums search the Internet for scrapbooks for newspaper clippings. A plethora of websites will give you all the help you need to find what you are looking for.

2. Paper tubes are wonderful for storing large drawings, poster art, etc. Charlie is an artist. From the time he started to draw, his doodles, drawings and later, his diagrams were of ships. His father and I thought he would pursue a career in technical drawing, but alas, he did not, but to this day, he still draws pictures of ships. So he has many drawings and overwhelmed at how they were all going to fit. So we laid out each and every one, unfurling them and making sure frayed edges were smoothed out and rips repaired. Then the drawings were lined up and firmly rolled back into place and slipped into the tube, date and contents noted.

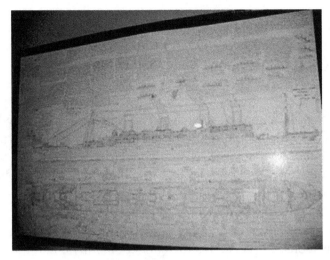

As he grew, so did the size of his drawings. The largest is a pencil and ink illustration of his most revered ship, the TITANIC. Charlie made multiple copies of this drawing. He even gave one to his high school teacher on his graduation day, and while he was a docent at our local maritime museum, he presented it to the director of the museum.

While doing this and before the copies were rolled up, I had Charlie take note of the TITANIC drawing hanging on his wall. I asked him if he saw any difference in the two drawings. At first he said no, but I told him to take a closer look at the writings in the picture. Getting close to it, he exclaimed, "Oh my, the writing is fading!" Yes, it sure was. So I explained how all artwork, be it a painting, photograph, reproduction work, etc., all fade with age and by light. Why do you think art museums take due-diligence protecting their art works? So now, with him taking care to preserve and protect his drawings, when the day comes and his TITANIC drawing has faded and no longer enjoyable to look at, he can slip the preserved one from out of the tube and replace the faded one, and once again enjoy his master piece.

4. Storing items that are not flat, such as booklets, brochures, maps, and in Charlie's case, maritime memorabilia, such as past ocean liner menus, programs, even tiny ashtrays, need to be preserved in a box that is used exclusively for that purpose. Called "Memory Boxes" they are available at craft stores and online. When you use these boxes, to help with organizing the items inside, keep to a theme, i.e.: travel, souvenirs, cards & letters, etc. Make sure fragile items are wrapped in tissue paper, photographs in slip covers, and then fashion a list of contents with dates, places, etc. And don't over-stuff the box. It won't close properly and the idea of preservation is mute.

Conservation, preservation, keeping, storing, organizing - all of these activities are well-worth the time and energy you put into it. And my Millennium is learning many life-long lessons as he sorts, selects, keeps & disposes of newspaper clippings, artwork, collections and then some. And he is actually enjoying this endeavor. He gets to visit times, places, and things buried in his closet and in his memory, but now has been unearthed and enjoyed again.

I have been reading too often how the baby boomer generation is discovering that many of their worldly possession, the ones they painstakingly saved and preserved to be passed down, are being disposed of by no other than their own children they wanted to pass it onto. How sad is that!

This seismic shift of stuff is underway in homes all over America and I am sure elsewhere in the world. Yes, it is true many of the Baby Boomer generation need and want to downsize their living space and give their things away. Unfortunately, many of the next generation; Millennials to be specific, don't want the large dining or master bedroom suite. It just doesn't fit into their transient life styles, small apartments or first homes.

Another aspect that is rather disturbing is how these young adults don't seem to want their own possessions either. School yearbooks, trophies, T-shirt collections, toys, and all those adorable baby clothes the parents hoped their child would dress their baby in. But why, I ask? What's wrong with revisiting those yearbooks? Why not save a few of those trophies they worked hard to get? Why not take all those quirky T-Shirts and fashion it into a useable item. And what about those baby clothes? Using them again saves money.

I recently read an article that said 20 & 30 year olds don't appear to be defined by their possessions, other than their latest-generation cellphones. That they live their lives digitally through Instagram, Facebook and YouTube, and that's how they capture their moments. That their whole life is on a computer. And how they don't need a shoe box full of greeting cards.

Even more distressing is how a 29-year-old estate marketer (I assume sells homes that will eventually be filled up with the very stuff she wants to get rid of, like old photos, bowls and cocktail glasses) would rather spend money on experiences. Just what does she think will help her remember these experiences if it isn't *stuff* . . . souvenirs from a distant land she visited, photos of loved ones and friends that passed on, precious things her family cherished over the generations. And if this isn't sad enough, her husband echoed, "I consider myself a

digital hoarder . . . if I can't store my memories of something in a computer, I'm probably not going to keep them around." I ask, how can these Millennials be so shallow? So short-sighted? So superficial? Is their family history meaningless? By time I got to the end of the article, I was fuming. When I read the last statement, I was downright smoldering.

A flippant professional organizer told a client, who should feel insulted, that the three large bags she filled of memories, one for each of her three sons . . . first-grade drawings or boxes with seashells glued to them . . . would not be appreciated. He said, "They made these things and gave them to you and you enjoyed them. The gift-giving cycle is now complete." How can this so-called

professional be so glib? So mindless? Perhaps he was never taught to appreciate gifts given and received? How will he feel when he is old and grey and finds he has no stuff left to reflect the life he lead. One thing for sure, he will have a difficult time healing from the initial loss of the tangible memories he gave away.

Genealogical Research

Boxes hidden or stored in the attic or basement can contain valuable information you may have never dreamed possible to discover. They may prove to be an invaluable wealth of knowledge when beginning a genealogical project. While some of the information is piecemeal and perhaps some of the contents divided between family sides, but there are probably enough clues to lead to others who have what you need and other potential sources. Listed below are additional items that you might find around your home that can help you create your genealogical history.

*Old family Bible with names and dates handwritten inside.
*Births, deaths and marriages dates recorded that occurred in the family over the years
*Birth certificates of great-grandparents, grandparents, parents, aunts, uncles, etc.
*Application for naturalization; books and papers associated with this history, a train ticket, ship manifest, and other travel documents
*Last Wills & Testaments; major and primary documents
*Military enlistment and discharge papers, medical records, group & individual photographs, weapons, uniforms, letters and postcards from military bases or units providing histories that put an individual at a particular place and time
*Licenses; old driver's licenses, professional licenses, or hunting/fishing licenses
*Property deeds, rental agreements, property records or census information
*Old newspaper clippings on current events, local politics, world happenings, weather *Handwritten business ledger with notes on prevailing business practices, contracts
*School records, report cards, papers, yearbooks, certificates of achievement, diplomas
*Religious items; baptismal, communion, confirmation, marriage certificates, burial Mass cards, obituaries
*Letters of all kinds: friendship, love, family correspondence that may yield valuable insight into the relationships, unique glimpses into personalities
*Scrapbooks; some of the most interesting and useful information can be found in these mementos that many people keep. They provide documentation of certain events in that person's life such as athletics, vacations, and entertainment. These certainly provide a unique peek into one's life and add wonderful anecdotes to a family history.
*Keepsakes; jewelry passed down from parent to child-each with its own story. Some have engravings that provide valuable clues, furniture, artwork, clothes, toys, books, etc.

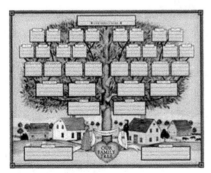

Study the history of your family . . . all sides . . . using whatever documents to discover the relationships between people. When you have all your ducks in a row, start a Family Tree. When that is finished, frame it by itself or incorporate into a shadow box where you can add small items that will lend more interest. And don't forget to involve the whole family; after all, it is their history, too.

Family Trees and DNA

We all have an ancestry, parentage and relations. We all have an origin; the foundation of our existence, and we all have a heritage, and it is this birthright and legacy we should all honor.

Before the computer age, when one wanted to look into family history, it was time-consuming and difficult at best. I have deep respect for all those who endeavored in their searches, making every effort to investigate and find their family's ancestry. Years ago my daughter and I visited Ellis Island to see if we could find any records on my Italian grandparents. Unfortunately, we did not. This whole movement to discover one's ancestry did not come together until the Internet and mostly until the online search engine, *Ancestry.com* became the investigative source. There are many other online sources as well.

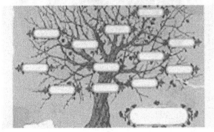

Parentage is the study on how a family is connected. The paternal & maternal lines and how they are all intertwined (like a tree, hence the Family Tree) can be mind-boggling. When backgrounds and pedigrees are established, a completer picture is created. But when these details are missing, one can get very lost as they climb those branches.

You will find a plethora of family tree charts that fit your needs on the internet. Print a few out so if mistakes or some confusion on dates, names, places, etc., should arise, you have a fresh tree to start growing your branches on. If a paper version of a family tree is not for you, you can create an online tree with genealogy computer software making it easier to organize, preserve and share your family history.

It is also a direct link to missing information about your roots. This project gets everyone involved and is especially rewarding for the young ones in the family to come to know and hear some stories about their relatives. So dig for your roots, collect those leaves, and find out who you are.

Family Trees and DNA

What is DNA? Deoxyribonucleic acid is a molecule that carries the genetic instructions used in the growth, development, functioning and reproduction of all known living organisms and many viruses. *Wikipedia*

Our origins are the stuff we are made of. Our roots, our beginnings and endings. Our DNA and RNA (chromosomes) and our genetic material. Where did we come from? What routes did we take to get where we ended up?

There is an ancestry program called *Geno 2.0 Next Generation Genographic Project Participation and DNA Ancestry Kit.* By participating you will discover the migration paths your ancient ancestors followed hundreds, even thousands, of years ago, with an unprecedented view of your ancestral journey.

My husband participated in *National Geographic Geno 2.0 Project* and was very surprised to discover his origins. He was amazed to find the long journeys his maternal family travel. Half his heritage is Norwegian, the other half German. As his mother was Norwegian, his upbringing was influenced by that culture more than German. But years later, he connected with his German relatives which extended our family circle.

I participated in *Ancestry.com DNA* research and was likewise surprised at the results. My maternal side is Italian; Paternal side Lithuanian. Throughout my childhood I heard many stories about the Italian family members, where they came from, where and why they settled in a particular place, and what they did for a living. I grew up learning very little about being Lithuanian, of which to this day, I have little knowledge about that culture. When my DNA results came in, I am more Lithuanian than I am Italian.

I had never been so surprised to find this out, which I am thrilled to have done, but unfortunately, I cannot share this discovery with my parents because they have both passed away. But now our children have mine and their father's DNA passed onto them, and we are making sure they will know and appreciate their genetic composition. It is very enlightening and this research becomes a part of your Family Museum.

Relations are another matter altogether. Connections, associations, links and lore, make interesting ties that bind.

"As long as the ties that bind us together are stronger than those that would tear us apart, all will be well."

However, we all need to work on our relations with family members. This can be accomplished by creating a *Family Museum* and preserve your material genealogy.

How would you feel if you did not know who your people were, what societies they belonged to, what customs and traditions and beliefs they passed down to you and from you to your family? Our ethnicities are who we are. A simple way to understand heritage is by observing your own traditions. What do you do for the holidays? What kind of food are you most familiar with? How do you decorate your home? What histories interest you? All of these and so much more is what your heritage is made up of. I discovered this site that really has a profound emotion to it. Never be afraid to discover you.

Collecting v. Saving

In the previous chapter, I touched lightly on a fact that is prevalent today: the frequent loss - either by choice or not - of family heirlooms. The focus of this book is to encourage saving, however, it is very unfortunate that the acts of dumping, ditching, discarding, and disposing of things, including family keepsakes created by the movements to down-size and unclutter one's life, is prevailing and needs to be reconsidered. And when one is uncertain as what to do and consults any of the many books out there that encourage such practices, such as *Collecting: An Unruly Passion: Psychological Perspectives:* by Werner Muensterberger, published in 1994.

Very briefly, the author interprets the acquisition of objects, "as a powerful help in keeping anxiety or uncertainty under control." This anxiety is ostensibly caused by "underlying factors" such as "war, a parent's suicide, prolonged illness, physical handicaps, death of a sibling, or simply not-good-enough early care."

How sad.

Then I was thrilled to read a review by Jeanette Hanisee Gabriel, formerly the Curator of mosaics at the Los Angeles County Museum of Art, Private Curator to the Rosalinda and Arthur Gilbert Collection in London and a consultant to Christie's and Sotheby's auction houses. She brings together Buyers and Sellers, and assists collectors wishing to authenticate, document, and value items in their collections. She wrote:

"I was offended from the first page of this book written by a psychiatrist, whose theory trivializes the emotional, aesthetic and intellectual (not to mention fun) qualities of collecting by reducing the pursuit to "compulsive action molded by irrational impulses."

Jeanette went on to say: *"With this tunnel-vision approach, Muensterberger proceeds to relate anecdotes of famous collectors' lives and interpret them as compulsive and unconscious behaviors to alleviate neuroses. The text is padded with details about the rich and famous: Balzac was a collector of "bric a brac," a hobby described as deriving from childhood suffering. The collecting habits of Holy Roman Emperor Rudolph II are similarly reduced to "anal-obsessive character traits." Getty, Duveen and a plethora of historical fugues litter the text. This book is a classic example of psychoanalytic gibberish, probably originating from the author's doctoral thesis, based on the number of footnotes.*

Ultimately, there is no argument here related to collecting that could not equally apply to any human behavior. Thus, there is no argument at all. As any educated person knows, it is all too easy to take an erroneous theory and find lots of examples to support it. As a former curator at a top ten museum, I think I am more familiar with collectors than the author. As a collector myself, I know that collecting is a happy, positive and enriching experience."

I agree. Collecting is a happy and enriching experience. However, unlike Europeans, people in the United States have few ties to their past. So perhaps it becomes more interesting and important to have things that create a past for us. According to Robert Thompson, a Ph.D. in the field of film and television at Syracuse University and president of the Popular Culture Association, *"In our consumer-oriented democratic, mobile, and rootless society; we are what stuff we have."* Thompson said: *"I turned 41 recently. If I want to create my own past, I can go to eBay or to a collectibles shop, find the things that were part of my past, and build up a museum of my personal life. There's something very satisfying about a personal, individual museum."* So start today, collecting and saving, and create a personal or Family Museum of your past for your future.

A brief note about Hoarding: Experts say people hoard for a variety of reasons. Items might carry emotional significance, such as remembering a happy time; examples from this book such as those written about "the times of your life." Or they may be thought of as being necessary at some point in the future. Family history, particularly important papers, books, photographs, even the old cookie jar your mom had are worth saving. It's not that these things are essential, they are options – choosing, selecting – all opportunities to preserve your heritage. Or the reason that holding onto these objects confers a sense of safety. Perhaps like the maxim, *safety in numbers*, which suggests that by being part of a large physical group or mass, an individual is less likely to be the victim of a mishap, accident, attack, or other bad event. Meaning that by not holding onto objects, they feel unsafe, therefore feeling securer with having stuff around. Security advisor Eleanor Everet said, "For safety is not a gadget but a state of mind." So in a hoarder's mind (I prefer calling them packrats, which according to Wikipedia, 'a Pack rat is a nest builder') they excessively accumulate and have a weakness to get rid of their possessions.

However, this subject matter has a positive side - the importance of collecting. The trick is to organizing the collections saved, to have respect for the things kept. Organization is the word. For example, pictured here are stacks of books, accumulated for a reason, but not respected. By taking the time to sort through, arrange, classify, categorize, and consolidate, these books will be in a better place and so will the collector.

Here are some useful tips to help yourself or someone you know that needs a few suggestions or a helping hand. First, be prepared for it to take time. Approach this task without judgement. Do not be quick to start throwing things away. Think about the connection to the object. Frame its value in terms of overall life. Start small, one room at a time. Examine each object. Once piles are established, decide which stays and which should go. You can also test the waters by having a neighbor or vice versa, keep things for a few weeks to see how that absence of those objects feels. There are many handbooks and organizational consultants that can offer advice and direction, but it is ultimately up to you. Be circumspect of the fine line between collecting and saving. Both have value, but that it up to you and how you organize and preserve what needs to be.

Last word. This picture shows a room stuffed to the gills with possessions. With all of the above suggestions, it is easy to see how some of these things can be better taken care of. For example the dollhouse. Depending on its condition, which much of it can be repaired if necessary, should be displayed somewhere in the home. I'm sure there are many stories that would be told if given the opportunity to do so. The artwork could be organized and a gallery wall can be created to better showcase this kept art collection. Sort through the bins and boxes and determine what stays and what goes. The room itself can be put to task, making it a Family Museum. All it takes is time and patience, and once everything is in a better place, you will feel better, too. After all, much of these things are memories that should be saved and shared.

Desirable Ownership

What is an antique? According to Wikipedia, it is an old collectable item. It is desirable because of its age, beauty, rarity, condition, utility, personal emotional connection, and/or other unique features. It is an object that represents a previous era or time period in human society. It is common practice to define "antique" as applying to objects at least 100 years old.

The Hunt is on . . . Antiquing is the act of shopping, identifying, negotiating, or bargaining for antiques. People buy items for personal use, gifts, or profit. Sources for antiquing include garage sales and yard sales, estate sales, resort towns, antique districts and international auction houses.

Be it hobby or a business, those who wish to start their own collection of prized antiques should first learn about the many different facets of antique collecting. Here are some tips that may be helpful.

1.) The most common feature of antiques is that they are remnants of the past. Their age may provide collectors with a good idea of their worth. The first thing as a general rule of thumb is to take their age into consideration.

2.) The time period on antique items is to target pieces that have been made on or before the 1830's. The reason for the year is that after the 1830's, most items were being mass-produced and therefore may have a selection of items that can be considered as prized antiques. This is not to say that items after that period aren't valuable. It is just that they may have different criteria for judging their value than earlier pieces.

3.) Focus on a certain type of antique to collect and then gather information as well as additional knowledge on how such pieces are being judged for their value. For example, if you are fond of collecting antique vases, then you should concentrate on collecting vases first before proceeding to other items. This will help make the beginner focus first on gaining knowledge about antique vases and how they are valued.

4.) Another tip is to seek the help of other experienced collectors especially when they come upon new items to add to their antique collection. Ask for input as well as suggestions as to how best to go about a new collection. Expert collectors may provide you with tips that they may want to share and impart some wisdom that you may not be able to get from books or any other source. Such expert advice could prove valuable as you begin to amass a sizable collection of antiques.

5.) Most importantly, whatever you collect, make sure you take every step in take great care of your treasurers. There is a plethora of websites that give excellent advice and have conservations and display products to sell. Part of enjoying antiques is preserving them. Don't forget that!

Our Family Museum is filled with collectibles. When an antique is considered so after 100 years of age, our things have about another half-century to go. But for what they are worth, their sentimentality is priceless. Our children's museum is filled with their treasures which are precious to them for

the worth they hold in memories of childhoods and young adult years. As like our collections, theirs will become more valuable with time. However, our family has a proud heritage and our Grandparents Museum is filled with antiques, not necessarily as defined as antique, but none-the-less, very dear to us. These two pictures are of my parents possessions and they are priceless to me. Here is a brief list and examples of categories desirable things to collect:

Americana (America's Culture)
Art (All types of medias)
Books (book-worms & bibliophiles)
China & Porcelain (fragile & delicate)
Coins (numismatics & collectors)
Collectibles (nostalgic & cherished)
Dolls (one of America's favorites)
 Coins (numismatics & collectors)
 Collectibles (nostalgic & cherished)
 Dolls (one of America's favorites)
Guns (proud collecting)
Jewelry (period & styles)
Knifes (mankind accomplishment)
Military (prideful deeds)
Miscellany (unusual collectibles)
Models (ageless collectors)
Other Stuff (creature collections)
Political Buttons (hobbyists & scholars)
Railroad (engineering collections)
Sports (cards & autographs)
Stamps (collectors & philatelist)
Toys (sentimentality collectors)
Watches & Instruments (mechanical art)

Everyone has an opinion. Many, particularly those in the field of analyzing human behavior, who, with my pedestrian knowledge on the study of the brain, have come to the conclusion that they are even still confused about the whys and wherefores as to why people collect, even after all their exploration and evaluations are through. Therefore, to simply state it, people collect and people save. It's only human nature that we do. So let's start out with an uncomplicated theory: *things give us comfort*.

Accumulation of things presents a tangible expression of a person or household. From the decorations hanging on the walls, to whose photographs are on display, and what collections are arrayed on mantelpieces. Material objects also help deal with loss and change and provide *comfort*. Collecting is also a great hobby. One can also learn about people through the medium of their things. There is a complex role played by objects in our lives, and indeed in our relationships with others. Becoming attuned to the presence of material forms can sometimes speak more easily and eloquently to the nature of relationships than can people themselves.

Does this make any sense to you? Kind of, you may think. Say, for example, you invite a new friend to your home and conversations are a bit awkward at first. Then you point out your collections of antique paper weights, each having a story to tell. Everyone had some kind of paper weight in their life and this subject may induce a lively conversation that will create a *comfort* zone. People like to tell stories and people like to hear them as long as you involved them by asking questions about their collections.

So what do you collect? And why do you collect? When people think of collecting, they may imagine expensive works of art or historical artifacts that are later sold to a museum or listed on eBay. The truth is, for many people who amass collections, the value of their collections are not monetary but emotional —and often, not for sale. Collections allow people to relive their childhoods, to connect themselves to a period in history or to a time they feel strongly about.

Their collections may help keep the past present, creating a *comfortable* atmosphere in which to live. However, do you feel overwhelm with stuff, fear that you are more connected to your material possessions more so then your relationships with people? That the more materialistic you become the more superficial you are, and that your relationships with people suffer as a result? Hogwash! The opposite is true; that possessions often remain profound and usually the closer our relationships are with objects, the closer are relationships with people."

Collectors are really happy people. Collecting is still mostly associated with positive emotions. There is the happiness from adding a new find to the collection, the excitement of the hunt, the social camaraderie when sharing their collection with other collectors. It is the *comfort of things*.

Excerpt from, *"The Comfort of Things,"* written by Daniel Miller; Cambridge: Polity, 2008

Memory Boxes
for Greeting Cards

Oh, the memories! With each and every greeting card I opened, a flood of recollections hit me like a 'ton of bricks.' Most of them brought a smile to my face, others made me laugh, and those with words of congratulations, support, and love brought on much reflection. Then I asked myself, do I hold onto these cards and letters? At the time I wrote this I had no answer. So I put the cards away and thought about what to do later. Later came and here is what I did. I organized them.

First I separated the cards by subject matter. Then by person to whom the card went to. Then once again into groups; birthday wishes, holidays, etc. Then by chronological order. Time consuming - you bet. Sometimes I did this sorting at the same time watching TV, which made the task less daunting. After that, I went back through the cards and kept some and discarded others. At times my heartstrings played a melancholy tune, but most of the time I enjoyed reading the cards again. Why, you may ask, should you do all this work? Because it gives you the opportunity to revisit that moment in time

Next, I found a pretty box, sometime more than one per person; husband/dad, wife/mom, children, son/daughter, sibling(s)-brother/sister, and other family (parents/grandparents/relatives) and friends. Then I put a bow around each box and gave each family member their "Card Box" as a Christmas gift. You can't imagine the surprised look on their faces when they opened the box and found their old greeting cards, along with other memento, for example, photos, drawings and other keepsakes.

As they opened their boxes, I heard, "What's this? Cards from Papa?" "You mean you saved them?" "Oh my goodness! I remember this card." "Gee, thanks Sis for thinking about me." "Honey, I love you more today than yesterday, and I believe you still do," said my husband has his eyes glistened with happy tears.

Go buy some memory boxes and fill them up with cherished times long forgotten but now remembered!

I Wish I Would Have Kept . . .

I wish I would have kept _____ (fill in the blank).
I wonder where _____ (fill in the blank).
If only I had kept _____ (fill in the blank).
I wish I knew . . . you get the picture.

How many times have you asked yourself questions like these? Or how about this scenario: you are perusing an antique store. You spot something you recall your aunt had, or maybe your grandmother used. Suddenly, you are in the room with your aunt watching her try on a new hat she just bought. Or you are in the kitchen with your grandmother and she hands you that heavy rolling pin and instructs you to roll out the pie dough. Should of, would of, and could of.

The fill-in-the-blank examples are here to give you the model for setting up an outline that will help you create a list of items you may want to buy to start or add to your museum.

For example: my father loved to thumb through the 971 page (1966 issue) or more of both the Sears Roebuck and Montgomery Ward catalogs. I can remember him sitting at the kitchen table, the radio playing softly in the background, and a cup of coffee getting cold as he got engrossed in the catalog, particularly the tools. Dad couldn't have enough tools! And if it wasn't for my perspicacious and astute daughter, who at the young age of 12, spotted these musty, rag-tagged catalogs in my parents' attic and saved them. I certainly was not as perceptive as she was at that age. Probably because there were so many of these humongous catalogs around the house, I could care less about preserving them. But as time went by and these behemoth tomes eventually became obsolete, whatever remains of these once cherished books is all there is now and forever. So when I find one, I thumb through it and wish I was back at the kitchen table watching my father dream. . . Of tools.

I wish I had even just one more picture of my nana and nonno. But this is the only one I have. Elisabetha and Anthony immigrated from Italy in the 1890s', traveling in steerage on one of the hundreds of ships that set sail from ports of Italy, arriving at Ellis Island and other ports-of-call in the United States. Settling in Chicago, Nonno work on the railroad and nana ran a grocery store. They raised 13 children, several went to college and became teachers, one served in WWI, and one was a big-band leader. Not bad for coming to America with a few bags and trunks.

As Eleanor Roosevelt said, *"It takes as much energy to wish as it does to plan."*

Where Items Can Be Found for Your Museum
Diamonds in the Rough

As previously mentioned, that when you need things you want to display in your museum that you no longer have but would be nice to own to complete a story and image of a person or event that you want to display, here is a list of places that you can peruse to find want you want and where it may be. Look at your local and major newspapers in the Classified Section to find the places that are hosting these events.

The room is silent for a few seconds until the auctioneer bellows, "Do I have a bid?" Everyone is watching everyone, but the auctioneer waits for signs. A nod of the head, a finger placed on the side of the nose, a tug of the ear. Perhaps in the movies you will see these actions.

At real auctions, people hold up signs with a number telling the auctioneer they are placing a bid. And the pace can catch the unwitting customer into buying something they don't want or can afford. Welcome to the world of Auctions. Like crossing a street, you look, listen, then cross. In this case, bid. There is so much information you need to know and understand before you go to an auction if you are going to participate. If not, they are fun and exciting to watch.

My experience with auctions came years ago when I lived in St. Petersburg, Fl. A century ago, many wealthy people from up north would come down during their harsh winters and put up second homes. They also traveled extensively on world tours, buying exquisite artifacts from foreign countries, decorating their residences with antiquities. Many years later, as time turn the tides, this generation of people died off, resulting in a treasure trove of fine things that eventually ended up on the auctioneer's block.

While I lived in Florida, I had a small art gallery offering visual art and antiques. I attended estate auctions looking for items for my gallery. I also found things I kept for myself, like the ring and this wood sculpture of a Persian House god.

At some auctions there are listings for "Box Lots," in which miscellaneous items are thrown together; no particular value given on them. The fun of bidding on it is that you get all the items. You never know; there may be that *diamond in the rough*. I found this fascinating original ink drawing of a woman slaying a serpent-like dragon.

There are many types of auctions and one that most people are familiar with is the Silent auction. A variant of the English auction in which bids are written on a sheet of paper. At the predetermined end of the auction, the highest listed bidder wins the item. This auction is often used in charity events.

Another rather rough-and-tumble source of fining what you are looking for, albeit it being a grab bag instead of an individual selection, is during auctions held at storage units. When rent is not paid on a storage locker for several months, the contents can be sold by an auctioneer as a single lot of items in the form of a cash-only auction. I have never attended one of these auctions. I would rather take the time to look through it all before I would bid on the item. I think it would behoove the owner of the things to be more circumspect about how and where they store their treasures, for perhaps there is a precious but forgotten heirloom.

Online Auction Sales are another source of where you can find, bid and buy antiques. A review by *Leah Stone* asks why use Online Auctions? She says, "Online auction sites provide a multitude of opportunities for entrepreneurs and bargain shoppers alike. Selling online allows you to supplement your income, or simply save money for that dream vacation. Additionally, thanks to today's auction sites, finding rare items has never been easier. With Internet shopping on the rise, online shoppers have been flocking to auction websites by the millions and their numbers are on the rise. But be careful. Learn more about them before you let your fingers to the bidding.

Auctions are fun, entertaining and edifying. But before you go, brush up on auction terminology, manners and mores. Check out websites that explain the aspects of the auctions as well as auction houses websites. It is best to be as prepared as you can be before the auctioneer says,

"Going once, going wide, SOLD to you!

Where Items Can Be Found for Your Museum
Diamonds in the Rough –At an Estate Sale

On a misty Friday morning, my daughter and I went to check out an Estate Sale. The home was of a prominent family and the sale was being held in the house itself. The ad in the local paper read:

First-in-line
First-Thru-the-Door.
Historic Sale in a Historic area!

For sale were 18th & 19th Century Furniture & Antiques, China, Porcelain, Oriental Rugs, Antique Toys & Christmas ornaments, collectibles, postcards, and much more. Parking in the historic area was limited, but we knew where the house was and where to find parking. So off we went, umbrella in hand. When we got there, about a dozen people were already in line, umbrellas soaked with rain. As we waited, we observed the deteriorating condition of the recently constructed home. In fact, we saw it being built in 1996.

As we waiting, conversations among the crowd were friendly. My daughter asked the lady standing next to her if she knew the family. "Absolutely," she stated. "My family and theirs were friends for many, many years. The owner was a well-known building contractor. He built this house." I could read my daughter's mind as we both looked at the peeling paint on the windows, wondering if he was such a fine builder, why was his house in need of repair." I soon found out the reason.

As she continued to talk about the family and taking much pride in her knowledge of them, I asked her if she knew the reason for the estate sale. Her face became somewhat melancholy when she said the couple were both deceased. With a quick recovery from the brief glum mood, I asked her if she knew why everything in the house was for sale. Were there not family members that should have been given these antiques? Emphatically she replied, "Oh! There are three children and they had already taken what they wanted!" What was left I guess they didn't want. And goodness me, the things they left behind made me

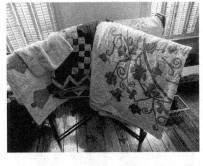

question not only why, but what were the things they did keep? As we finally gained access into the house . . . two had to leave before two more would be let in, we were directed to go into the formal living room still filled with many pieces of fine furniture. Most of it still nice but worn. You could tell that the residents of the home were wealthy and had exquisite taste.

Next room was the formal dining room, paneled from ceiling to floor, and must have been the site of many fancy dinners. The table had stacks of beautiful china, glassware, and tablecloths. On a small table were a selection of old books. As my daughter is a bibliophile at heart, she was thrilled when she found a child's school book she had to have. I have plenty of dishes and glassware, so off we went into the kitchen. You could tell that it was a serious culinary center, counters and cabinets everywhere. Again, piles of dishes, rows of crystal glasses, many colorful vintage Depression glass, all there for the buying. Nothing here for us, so we stepped down on thru the long hall into the family room.

There was an entire wall of shelves with more china, porcelain antiques, knick-knacks, books, statuary, candlesticks, etc. On a large table, silver platters, teapots, and more dishes. There were two massive chests, a large glass curio cabinet, two wooden armchairs and a very fine card table. With all that furniture, one would wonder if there was room for people. Again, nothing we wanted, so up the stairs we went and directed into a bedroom.

Here tables of toys reigned, evidence that there were children in this family and the builder husband/father created dollhouses, cradles and toy furniture. Boxes of Christmas items filled several tables. The children must of love reindeer because there had to be at least eight boxes of them alone. In the dressing room were more boxes of Christmas tree glass ornaments, many vintage and very collectible. I even looked for one particular ornament I remember has a kid, but have yet to find it.

Where Items Can Be Found for Your Museum
Diamonds in the Rough –At an Estate Sale

The only thing I found that I wanted was a miniature replica of the famous statue of the *Three Graces*. My daughter bought it for me.

Finished with our hunt, we went back downstairs to pay for our finds. While my daughter waited in line, I looked around and felt the sad emptiness and silence that was soon to be in this house once filled with children, dinner parties and life. Sales like these make me sad. Even though the descendants got what they wanted, none of them wanted to keep the house. It was being sold after the sale. If one of them kept the house, that bookcase in the family room would have made a perfect *Family Museum*. It could have had some of those vintage toys, a few of those gorgeous dishes, photographs and antiques on display. But it was not meant to be. So back out into the misty weather and home to blog about the estate sale.

Next time you read about one of these sales, go to it. Do not be intimidated by the hoity-toity and snooty sounding moniker. The estate sale manager hired by the family is there to organize and sell. Many times the things that remain are transferred to another sale called an Estate Auction. The purpose of these sales is to make as much money for the seller as it is for the owner. But you never know when someone missed and you found a *diamond in the rough*. Happy Hunting!

Antique stores and malls are shopping meccas that provide the opportunity for buyers to browse through a wide range of items that are considered to be collectibles.

Individual antique stores usually deal with a certain type of collections, such as art or clothing, catering to particular tastes. For example, a single store is likely to carry the more predictable items such as beds, dressers, and sofas, whereas an antique mall with its usual wide range of selections is likely to have hard to find items like fainting couches, original wood burning stoves, tapestries, and even authentic period clothing from eras gone by. Both cater to collectors and browsing through either provide hours of edifying enjoyment.

 While many may think that an antique mall would be an expensive place to shop, the fact is that many items carried in malls are very affordable. Some of the items are not restored, making them attractive  bargains. There is usually an array of old books, costume jewelry, and knick-knacks that tend to be low-ticket items. Some are now selling vintage vinyl records, making the mall attractive to yet another generation of customers.

Yet there is one very good attribute that comes out of these emporiums of memories, and that is they may have what you are looking for. Something to replace the one that was lost, given away or trashed. You can find just about everything and when you do and place it in your *family museum,* it either tell or enhance your story. And another feature these antique merchants give are lessons in how to display. Study the cabinets, the shelving, and the lighting. Notice the careful placement and eye-catching presentations.

Have fun going down memory lane, even though you may feel a bit melancholy. That feeling can make you actually feel grateful for the things you did save. So go on. Visit an antique store or mall, talk with the dealers. Appreciate the service they provide and then go home and fill *your family museum* with memories.

As they say, one person's trash is another's treasure.

Pick up any newspaper and there is a section for many weekend yard and garage sales. Some are listed individually, others are listed as Multi-Family Yard Sales, Moving Sales, Flea Markets, and some get fancy and call them Residential Estate Sales. Some will be specific, such as one ad that stated the

sale was a Craft & Sportsman Show. How did a "show" get listed among the sales? I guess it doesn't matter, so whatever the event is called, you will find a plethora of things, some you need, others you want, and for that main reason you search out these sales; the bargain awaits.

Some newspaper yard sale pages have a Locator Map. Depending on how much time you have, how far you are willing to travel, and how much money you want to spend, it is wise to map out the routes and locations. Some of these excursions can be strenuous, so read what each sale has to offer. For instance, say you are looking for toys. For a toy to be classified as an antique, the ad may read, *vintage* toys.

The first ad offering toys is the moving sale. Not detailed at all and just the address is given. Look for it on the locator map, but the street name is not there. How can you find this place? No phone number either, so perhaps you do not go there. Check that one off the list. Letting your fingers do the walking, find an ad that lists antiques, furniture, porcelain dolls, etc. Now this looks promising. But once again, you can't locate the street on the map and no phone number. Frustrated but not giving up, you continue your search.

You find in bold print the word **HUGH** Yard Sale with explicit directions, and it lists toys! Though there was still no phone number, the address was clear and you found it on the map. Then you look at the next ad and you can tell the person who was conducting the multi-family yard sale knew what he/she was doing. It read, "Balloon on mailbox." Now how clever is that. The ad even gives which entrance to use when entering the sub-division. Smart, indeed. Then you found more toys in the next ad and this one, too, gave good directions.

Along with the fancy Residential Estate Sale ad, there was another unusual yard sale. This one said, in bold type, **REMODELING SALE.** The ad went on to say, NO EARLY BIRDS! Limited Quantity, Cash Only! Immediate Removal Required. Wow! Lots of rules. And no wonder why. It was some sort of resort that was obviously doing some updating. Sure there were many bargains there, but not interested in beds and furniture. However, these sales a good for that purpose and you never know what else you might find.

Then the Estate Sale ad caught your eye because it listed "doll collection." Now here may be a good place to start your trip. You got to start somewhere and the sooner you get to where you want to go, there is more opportunity to find the good stuff. The following ad is explicit. **"The Best is First, Sat. 7am – 2 pm**. Like the old adage, *First come, first serve*. Or this one, *The Early Bird gets the worm*. So when you plan your yard sale search, do so days in advance. That way, you have a good chance at succeeding.

P.S. As I was looking for yard & garage sale signs on Google Images, I came across another moniker for this type of merchandise sale. It is called a **Rummage Sale.** Now I haven't heard that word it years and laughed when I saw it. The word rummage means, (slang, U.S.) search, hunt, ransack, scour, look everywhere, look high & low, leave no stone unturned. Along

with printed ads, there are a many websites for you to find the sale that most interests you. And remember that whatever reason brings you to these sales, you are looking for that special something for you *Family Museum*. Good luck!

Where Items Can Be Found for Your Museum
Diamonds in the Rough – Pawn Shops

To conclude *Diamonds in the Rough*, the subject is on the ancient practice of pawning. When I started to research this topic, I was overwhelmed with how much information there is on the Internet. I personally have not dealt with pawn shops, so I will let the experts guide you. But for intents and purposes, I thought a little history would be interesting.

Let's start with Queen Isabella. If it wasn't for her and her husband, Ferdinand, who supported and financed Christopher Columbus' 1492 voyage, he would not have discovered the "New World." More in depth history can be found on Wikipedia.

The story about the pawnbroker's symbol is just as interesting. The three sphere symbol is attributed to the Medici family of Florence, Italy. Most European towns called the pawn shop the "Lombard." The House of Lombard was a banking community in medieval London, England. According to legend, a Medici employed by Charlemagne slew a giant using three bags of rocks. The three-ball symbol became the family crest. Since the Medici's were so successful in the financial, banking, and money lending industries, other families also adopted the symbol. The three golden spheres hung in front of the merchant's houses, and not the arms of the Medici family. It has been conjectured that the golden spheres were originally three flat yellow effigies of byzants, or gold coins, laid heraldically upon a sable field, but were converted into spheres to better attract attention. Throughout the middle Ages, coats of arms bore three balls, orbs, plates, discs, coins and more as symbols of monetary success. Pawnbrokers (and their detractors) joke that the three balls mean "Two to one, you won't get your stuff back."

Saint Nicholas is the patron saint of pawnbrokers. The symbol has also been attributed to the story of Nicholas giving a poor man's three daughters each a bag of gold so they could get married. Don't you just love history? Stories about people, places and things is in fact, what you do when you create your *Family Museum,* assembling your family heirlooms, displaying your collections, and preserving your antiques. And when you need to add to your museum, you may find it in a pawn shop.

As I researched sites about pawnshops and how to use them, I read that more Americans are going to Pawn shops to get fast cash by selling jewelry, electronics, tools and other personal items. According to data from the National Pawnbrokers Association, there now are 11,000 pawn shops in the U.S. Need to sell or want to buy? Check out a Pawn Shop. It could be very interesting.

What Should Be Saved - The Times of Your Life

The days and years of a life zip by so quickly, but when you are in that moment, life just happens. You go about your daily living, sometimes impervious, unaffected by the passing of that time, and then here you are, looking through boxes stacked wherever and wonder where did all that time go.

Sad but true that we can't stop time, however, we can remember it by simply saving something, anything, that invokes a memory, an event, person and experience that shaped your life. Sure there are instances you rather forget, need to forget, but there are probably more that should be remembered, preserved and passed on. So the question is, "What should be saved?" Things from the times of your life.

Such as Clothing: That special dress or uniform. Think vintage. Think precious. Recall the time it was worn and who wore it. Think about passing it down and have fun wearing it again. Use your imagination when displaying it: Hang or prop it up, attach or place items affiliated with it, such as shoes & accessories. Place a photo of it being worn.

Did you save those special T-Shirts? (I did! Boxes of them). Organize shirts by size and subject matter such travels, school events and hobbies. Then make a simple T-Shirt Quilt or pillows. These make great gifts.

How about Furniture: highchairs, Baby and doll cradles, Toy boxes, rocking horses, Tables & chairs, and rugs. How about any one of the many cell phones, even beepers (remember those)?

Why do we keep these? Because like many things in our Family Museum, they tell the story of invention, innovation & revolution, advancement, improvement & modernism. Can you imagine going back to only one phone in the house? Can you imagine having to wait until you got home to talk to whomever you need to converse with?

My favorite is this big old red push-button phone. It required a land-line and had a great loud ring, and the best feature is when you really wanted to hang up on someone, you can do it with gusto. Bang! Take that!

Scrapbooking is a method for preserving personal and family history in the form of a scrapbook.

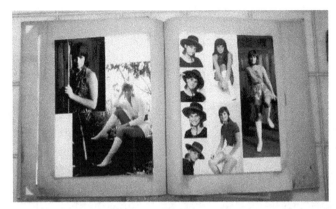

Pictures for Modeling Composite

Autograph, photograph, stamp, sticker, wedding, baby and more are subjects for scrapbooks. Do you have one or several? And where are they now? There are many in our family museum, but sadly not on display because of their sizes.

Here is some history about Scrapbooking from Wikipedia: In the 15th century, commonplace books popular in England, emerged as a way to compile information that included recipes, quotations, letters, poems and more. Each commonplace book was unique to its creator's particular interests.

Additionally, friendship albums and school yearbooks afforded girls in the 18th and 19th centuries an outlet through which to share their literary skills and allowed girls an opportunity to document their own personalized historical record previously not readily available to them.

The advent of modern photography began with the first permanent photograph created by Joseph Niepce in 1826. This allowed the average person to begin to incorporate photographs into their scrapbooks. They also often included bits of memorabilia like newspaper clippings, letters, etc.

Marielen Christensen is often credited with turning scrapbooking from what was once just the age-old scrapbook hobby into the actual industry containing businesses devoted specifically to the sale and manufacturing of scrapbooking supplies. She began designing creative pages for her family's photo memories, inserting the completed pages into sheet protectors. By 1980, she had assembled over fifty volumes and was invited to display them at the World Conference on Records in Marielen and her husband A.J. authored and published a how-to book, and opened a scrapbook store in Spanish Fork in 1981 that remains open today.

These days, scrapbooking can be done in so many ways. You can use beautiful colored paper, stickers, drawings, photos, and so many other supplies. Scrapbooking is like a visual diary, capturing all your creativity, thoughts feelings, and memories in a book.

As we are now in the age of the download and the hard drive, the photography book is currently thriving as a medium, making the old-fashioned photo album a thing of the past. Yet, many people still desire a physical object that can be held, paged through again and again, and shown to others. Today, the photo album has given way to the self-published photo book, an online publishing phenomenon that means you or I can create our own album using preordained templates and printed from digital files.

The thing about digital is it allows us to take many photos cheaply and then view them on a PC or TV, making it possible to have a whole family archive on a single flash drive. But what happens to stored images when computer systems change? A picture is always a picture, a digital image is just so many 0's and 1's. So what happens in years to come if computers can't "read" today's binary notation? You make digital back-ups of old photo albums to preserve them for future generations. Too often photo albums are lost, damaged, or dispersed. With digital media, a person's many descendants can all have a copy of old photographs.

Still, the photo album survives. They have an integrity that digital storage cannot capture.

Creating photo collections takes time, so do it in stages. As you go through the photos, ask yourself these questions: Do I recognize the person? Do I find the photo of the subject(s) flattering? Do I like the person? Do I have fond memories of the event? Do I have more than one copy of this photo? Have a family member or friend assist you. It can actually be fun as you reminisce about old times, cry a little bit over lost friends or family members, and look back at the places you lived and visited, etc. And cackle all you can when you deep-six some images of yourself that you would rather not bestow on posterity.

As you create your photographic album, try not to eliminate the accidental, the blurred the botched, faded and crumpled photographs. These images document ordinary life and are windows to the past.

The process of creating an old-fashioned, hand-crafted albums is an abiding desire to tell a story with photographs which will keep album-making alive. When you hold a photo album, you sense that you are in possession of something unique, intimate, and meant to be saved for a long time. As you turn the pages and look at the images, you take in the maker's experience, invoking your imagination and prompting personal memories.

So as you find packets of photos in drawers and boxes throughout your home, spend a few minutes recalling the moment. Then preserve them. And for those digital images, once they are edited, don't forget to look at them.

Here are a few pages of photographs from my family's albums.

Goesel Family Albums

In May 1995, we went to Disney World in Florida. Charlie was nine years old, the best age a kid could be to enjoy all the sights of sounds of Disney's Magic Kingdom. Mickey Mouse graces the cover of this album, stock full of photos of Charlie and his grandmother, mom & sister. Not only are there pages of pictures, there are all sorts of fun items like menus, coloring pages, puzzles, and drawings. A lot of fun to look at and revisit those magic moments.

When we lived in Florida, we had a swimming pool in our backyard. With the weather being hot in the spring, summer and fall, a pool is not a luxury, it is a necessity especially if you don't live near the water. This album is full of pictures of Tiffeni with her school friends. They love to come home with her after school, swim and stay over for a slumber party. Even our dog Sidney enjoyed the pool, chasing a ball around. Many pool parties and family gathering were held by the pool. Great memories, one and all.

These two pages of Lizzie's black & white photographs shows many stages of her childhood. From baby, to learning how to walk, ride a tricycle, going to the beach, playing in the mud, going off to school, all of these moment are milestones that should be remembered, only if I could. The only way I know of what was going on in these pictures are what my parents have told me, and they must have been entertaining for them to capture the moments.

Keith enlisted in the Naval Reserves in 1972. He had a long and prosperous naval career, and after 29 years of service, he retired as a Chief Petty Officer. HE worked in many areas doing a variety of jobs, cumulated as a Career Counselor. He traveled to many foreign countries, met with many dangerous situations, forged many friendships, and gain a confidence that served him well throughout his career. Many of his ribbons and medals are in the Family Museum and he takes great pride in seeing and sharing them.

What Should Be Saved - The Times of Your Life
Charm Bracelet

I believe in memory and the way objects are understood to hold memory, to tell stories and act as place markers. That is not only what a *Family Museum* is all about, a Charm Bracelet does the same – it holds memories. What makes them endearing is that there is a story contained in each and every one of those charms as they artfully jingle and dangle from wrists. Now back in fashion and very trendy.

When I was a child, I admired and longed to touch the sparkly charms swinging from silver or gold bracelets adorning fashionable women. I do not recall seeing such bracelets on my relatives or my mother's wrist, but I do remember a stylish friend of hers having one in gold. She was rather wealthy, therefore, could afford such a collection of bubbles. I would have loved to of asked her questions about the origin and meaning of her charms, but alas, I was much too shy. Then one day my wish came true.

When I turned sixteen, my parents bought me a charm bracelet affixed with a collection of tiny trinkets that had absolutely no meaning or connection to me. The one and only befitting was the *Sweet 16* Heart. The charms that still baffle me today are the ice cube tong, a cylinder cage with a pair of dice, a tambourine, and a basket of flowers, a dagger, a wish bone and a cat. The cat I understand because I had several cats that drove my mother crazy. As time went on, charms that told of the important moments to me found their way onto my bracelet. My husband loved buying charms for me because they spoke a silent language of love. Eventually, my children bought me charms. That's really what my charm bracelet is; a miniature storybook of my life. Now my bracelet is full of charms from the places I've visited, a myriad of milestones and other meaningful events and people who are woven into the fabric of my life. And it's not finished, as my story is still being told.

The charm bracelet is a piece of jewelry so reflective of its wearer that it doubles as a figurative profile. I think that it is a bit of a disappointment that charm bracelets are not more explicitly defined as *memory bracelets* because it tells the story of a life. As the purpose of this book is to encourage the preservation of family history, the charm bracelet can be used as a narrative device. Here's a suggestion: if your Mother or Grandmother has a vintage charm bracelet, have them tell the stories their charms reveal. And have them do it in front of a video camera. This could be an incredible and easy way to gather and collect a part of their history that might otherwise be lost.

What Should Be Saved – The Times of Your Life
Charm Bracelet

If you have a charm bracelet, look at it with new eyes. This is your story, a literal scrapbook of your life. Now, if you do not have one and always wanted one, it is never too late to start collecting the charms that represent your lifetime. You can either start with brand new gold or silver charms available at jewelry stores. The latest design in charm bracelets is the Pandora Bracelet with its threading system and high-quality charm selection. They are a bit bigger than the traditional charms. Or you can go to an antique store and be overwhelmed by a plethora of vintage charms, some still attached to the chain bracelet or for sale individually. There is also an abundance of charms and bracelets available online.

Elegant, classy and fun, Charm Bracelets are a great way to make your own individual fashion statement. They are for the most part not name branded, or designer themed, and not all current and vintage charms are gold or silver. There is a variety of others such as copper, brass, celluloid, plastic, wood, stones, gems, etc. You can collect an eclectic mix of charms representing your favorite hobbies, keeping them as spaced or as packed as you please, or you can search for charms of a single motif based on a theme, such as a Christmas bracelet. Or they can even be a wacky.

For example, this one made from miniature foodstuffs. Charm bracelets can have a great sense of humor! So have fun putting a charm bracelet together for yourself as well as someone you love.

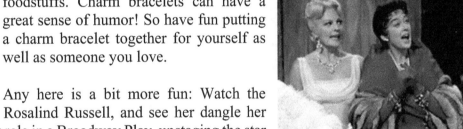

Any here is a bit more fun: Watch the movie *"Auntie Mame"* starring Rosalind Russell, and see her dangle her charm bracelets has she plays her role in a Broadway Play, upstaging the star and closing the show on its first night. What a hoot!

What Should Be Saved - The Times of Your Life
School Days

First a little history: The best known part of this song is its chorus:

School days, school days, Dear old Golden Rule days,
"Reading and 'riting and 'rithmetic, Taught to the tune of the hick'ry stick.
You were my queen in calico, I was your bashful, barefoot beau,
and you wrote on my slate, "I Love You, Joe" When we were a couple o' kids.

Do you remember singing this song? I don't really except the first three lines. Yet the nostalgia this song imparts will always remain in collective consciousness until those generations who do have passed on. And just for kicks, when I use to complain about the long walk to the school bus stop, my father would repeat once again, "Lizbit. I use to walk miles in the snow to get to school…" and then I said, "Ya, I know. And you use to write on the back of s shovel." He laughed.

All this may seem strange, but it really wasn't that long ago that kids walked miles to school and depending on where you lived, particularly in the country on a farm, school days were determined by the farmer's crops. Here is a short story for why kids go back to school the day after Labor Day:

Kids didn't always have summers off. Summer vacation as we know it is a pretty recent phenomenon. When the public education system started in the 1800s, calendars varied depending on the needs of the community. In cities, schools were open practically year-round, up to 240 days a year. Rural schools, on the other hand, were open for only about five months over two sessions, in the winter and summer. Fall and spring, school was out so children could help harvest the crops and help with planting. This does not apply today. In fact, many school begin in August.

In our Family Museum there are many things that bring back school day memories. A picture of Keith with his High School Sports Letters, Lizzie's school books, Tiffeni's cool denim jacket, and Charlie's lunch box.

We all have memories of school days. And if you have anything from those years, don't keep them in boxes. Take some time and rediscover those papers, artworks, photographs, even perhaps a few souvenirs like sports letters, yearbooks, trophies, report cards. These all mark life's paths, rites of passage, experiences, etc. This history is your history. Be proud of it. Show it off. Share it with others and have them share theirs with you. Happy School Days to You!

Do you still have your high school yearbooks? Where are they now: in the attic or basement? When was the last time you looked at them? Are you still in touch with any of those friends you made during your high school years?

Do you remember when you first got your yearbook how you scanned every page to see how many pictures there were of you? As I look through my book it made me recall how I missed out on a lot of extracurricular activities, even though I remember participating. In fact, the only club I belonged too, my picture was cut out. Go figure.

Your yearbook provides a plethora of information about the life you led during your school years. The photographs pretty much tell the story, but also the personal autographs everyone hustled to get as soon as the year books were distributed. Remember rushing about between classes, at lunch, before and after school? And why were they so important? I even remember the process being a bit of a competition. Who could get the most autographs. And why was it so important that the corners of the pages be the place to write those words of good luck and best wishes? I guess it really doesn't matter as long as your friends cared enough to write some last words to you.

Keith's Senior Picture Stats: Basketball 1,2,3,4; Cross Country 3; Hall Monitor 4; Homecoming Committee 3; Intramural 1,2,3,4; National Honor Society 3,4; Prom Committee 3

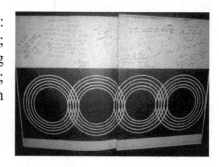

Keith's Autographs: *Keith, It was fun in College Prep – even though you did cut me down all the time! Good Luck! Love, Char Jo; Keith, You're the best d _ _ _ (you said dirty) hall monitor around. I'll never forgive you for snitching on me – just because I threw your book in the garbage can – Well anyway – Luck! Friends Always, Joyce Mitchell '68; Dear Keith, To one of the greatest guys I've ever known. I wish you luck at school and in your live forever. Just stay as sweet as you are now. Love Always, Deb; To Keith, One of the greatest basketball players I know. Duschean*

Lizzie's Senior Picture Stats: F.H.A. (Future Homemakers of America) 1; F.B.L.A. Future Business Leaders of America) 3,4

Lizzie's Autographs: *Liz, It sure was nice having you in shorthand class even if you never had an eraser or any typing paper. Good luck always in everything you do. Be god this summer but still have fun!! Love ya, Mary '68. Liz, I would like to think of something different to say but all I can think of is that you're a wonderful girl with lots of laughs and I hope you never change. There is far too few people like you around. Hope we do get together soon, and I'm sure we will. Good Luck in the future and may you never stop smiling. (Besides you have sexy teeth). Right? Right! Love Jerry; Liz, You certainly are very talented in the dance area and I hope you continue with it after school. I hope the future brings you all the happiness and success in the world. Miss VanDeWalle; Liz, You are my finest dance student and I really enjoyed having you in class. Best wishes in the future especially modeling. I'll be looking for you in Vogue. Mrs. Robison*

Your yearbooks, not just from High School, but grade, junior, college, etc., should go into your family museum, along with your class pictures and class ring, any trophies or awards you received, and any other item that will make it fun to recall those glory days of education. Share it all with family and friends and remember the good times!

FYI: The people at Ancestry.com did some research on Yearbooks titled, "About U.S. School Yearbooks." It is an indexed collection of middle, junior, high school and college yearbooks from across the United States. Their take on how a yearbook relates to ancestry (genealogical research) is this: yearbooks are a source of many details, especially when you are searching for names and dates, times and places, what you/they looked like, even world events, fads, and pop culture.

The Class Ring (also known as a graduation, graduate, senior, or grad ring) is a ring worn by students and alumni to commemorate their graduation, generally for a high school, college, or university.

The *Complete Book of Etiquette* by Amy Vanderbilt indicates the following protocol for wearing of a class ring: For as long as the wearer is in school, the insignia should face the wearer to remind him/her of the goal of graduation. Upon graduation, the class ring gains the status of a "badge of honor" similar to a diploma, with the effect that graduation entitles the wearer to display the insignia facing outward so that it faces other viewers. An additional justification for this practice is the rationale that the ring also symbolizes the graduate him/herself: During the wearer's time in school, she or he focuses on self-development and goals specific to the insular academic environment; upon graduation, the wearer enters the wider world and puts what s/he has learned to work in shaping it.

A notable exception to this protocol is the custom to wear the rings on the left hand in observance of the ancient belief, which also underlay the Anglo-American and Jewish custom of wearing wedding bands on the left hand, that a vein connects the left ring finger to the heart.

This history is interesting, but what is more notable is how the ring was used in announcing that you were *"going steady!"* Remember that? When a gal and guy professed their love for each other, they gave one another their class ring. (An exception here is if there was an age gap . . . the guy was a junior or senior and the gal was a freshman or sophomore, which meant they did not have class rings yet). The guy would usually wear it on a chain around his neck because the ring was too small for his finger. The gal used several creative ways to wear the large ring. Most popular way was to wrap a fuzzy angora yarn (colors varied) around the back of the ring to make it fit on her finger. I can't tell you how many gals I saw wearing this humongous ring on their tiny hand. And the ring would clunk against the desk, and the fuzzy yarn would look terrible when it got wet.

I also remember witnessing volatile confrontations between the steady couple, when she would hank the ring off her finger and throw it at the most likely stunned guy. I wonder who took off the fuzzy yarn. Mom, perhaps.

When I was researching the history on class rings, I was sadden to read how many sources there are to help you get rid of your ring. Need money? Find out how much gold is in the ring, minus the stone, which apparently do not have much worth to them. Why would anyone want to sell their class ring, especially if it isn't going to result in a monetary windfall? This situation is what my blog is all about . . . preserving your history. And what better item can you name that represents a major time in your life where you can still recall both the good and bad experiences that shaped your life. Why not wear it one day and see how many conversations get started. If it doesn't fit, like mine doesn't, wear it on a chain or bracelet. Or just put it in your family museum, next to the yearbook and graduation picture.

Note on the maker of the Class Rings: Both were made by Harry Heriff and Randall Jones in 1920 located in Indianapolis, IN. They are still in business today.

Tried as I might, I could not remember where we went for our Senior Class Trip. All I could recall was some sort of beach and small amusement park. Living in Illinois, there were many lakes, so I knew it had to be one of them.

As I write my blog, I am constantly consulting my husband Keith. He seems to remember things I don't. So I asked him and he knew right away. It was Bass Lake in Indiana. "How did you know that?" Laughing he says, "We went there several years ago." Stunned, I asked, "When?" Shaking his head at my memory loss, he replied, "Don't you remember when we all went up to see my cousin Paul and his family who have a cabin at that lake?" "Yes, but I don't remember the amusement park being there." He continued, "Paul said it was torn down years ago. He pointed out the area from his boat and you said you remembered it." "Well, by gosh by golly. I did, and then I started to remember the trip, and know why I forgot about it. I didn't have an exceptional good time. It was hot, the water was cold, and I wasn't particularly fond of scary rides. Most of all, I remember not having a boyfriend to enjoy this trip with me like most of the other gals did. Oh well, C'st la vie!

Then I asked Keith if he went t on a senior class trip. "Nope. Can't recall that we even had one."

Things had certainly changed a lot from the class trips of yore compared to today. Though our daughter, Tiffeni, graduated in 1988. Her class was very small since it was a private school and we lived in Florida. Back then Disney World use to host Senior Class Trip events for all the high schools in Florida for one night in June. She recalls the park closed early for the graduates, who then had the run of the place. She said she had a ball. Or son, Charlie, had an exceptional class trip as well. He was a Distant Learning Student with a school in California. The Graduation ceremony with a Prom the night before was at the school, so we all flew out there from Virginia. Being that Charlie did not know any of the other students, his sister was his prom date. They had a blast.

Class rings and class trips commemorate more than the end of the most influential four years in a person's life. The material ring perhaps can still be worn and the class trip memories recalled. Both should have a place in your family museum; the ring on display with your senior class picture and maybe a scrapbook with photos of the class trip. Again, these need to be preserved and handed down. And what fun you will have recalling these milestones in your live.

Do you still have your class ring and remember your senior class trip?

In the early days of high school proms, the night time dance served a similar function to a debutante ball. Early proms were times of first: the first adult social event for teenagers; the first time taking the family car out after dark; the first real dress-up affair; and so forth. Proms (promenade) also served as a heavily-documented milestone in which the participants were taking an important step into a new stage in their lives.

Proms worked their way down incrementally from college gatherings to high school extravaganzas. In the early 1900s, prom was a simple tea dance where high school seniors wore their Sunday best. In the 1920s and 1930s, prom expanded into an annual class banquet where students wore party clothes and danced afterward. As Americans gained more money and leisure time in the 1950s, proms became more extravagant and elaborate, bearing similarity to today's proms. The high school gym may have been an acceptable setting for sophomore dances (sock- hops), but junior prom and senior balls gradually moved to hotel ballrooms and country clubs. These days' limousines have become compulsory for the event.

Competition blossomed, as teens strove to have the best dress, the best mode of transportation, and the best looking date. Competition for the prom court also intensified, as the designation of "prom queen" became an important distinction of popularity. In a way, prom became the pinnacle event of a high school student's life.

My husband Keith and I graduated high school in 1968 but from different schools. When I asked him if he went to his senior prom, he emphatically replied, *"No!"* I had already known this as we have been married 44 years, but it was fun to ask him again. "Why," I teased. *"Money! Why would I spend my hard-earned money on a girl I didn't know or care to know?"* His response still surprises me because he was the "all-time campus great guy . . . Varsity Basketball Player of the Year, Honor Student, and darn right handsome. Even his best friend tried to convince him to go as a double-date. His snarky reply, *"Ah, right. You and her up in the front seat necking like crazy and me sitting in the back seat with some girl I did not want to kiss or anything else! Forget about it!"* Having gotten this off his chest once again, he said, *"Now if I had known you then, I would have taken you to the prom."* How sweet.

My high school was small by today's standards. My graduating class had less than 300 students. It was a very traditional high school. Perhaps this is not a common lexicon to use regarding schools. The reason I say this is because all the seniors received a very formal invitation from the Junior Class. It stated,

"The Junior Class of Lincoln-Way Community High School requests the pleasure of your company at the Junior-Senior Prom, Friday, the twenty-fourth of May at eight-thirty in the evening at the Chateau Bu-Sche in Oak Lawn, Illinois."

Wow! A formal invitation sent to me! It came in the mail and even had a smaller card in the envelope. Obviously it was not an R.S.V.P. card because I still have it. Never-the-less, it was quite something and impressive. I wonder if high schools today send out such lavish invitations.

Prom day was looming in fast and I waited until the last minute to be asked, but alas, I was not. So when push came to shove, I asked Don, a nice guy, very shy, but sweet as could be. He wore a white tuxedo, looking as uncomfortable as I am sure he felt. He presented me with the corsage; I pinned the boutonniere on his lapel. I can recall how he shook with nervousness.

My mother picked out my prom dress. I did not like the color (brown) but the style was in. A straight sleeveless crepe dress with a high-neck jeweled collar. I was really crazy about the shoes. They were a shiny brown patent with stack Lucite heels. Cool! A small clutch of some kind and not much jewelry. Pierced ears were not of the fashion yet, but bouffant hairdos where. All decked out, ready to go, but I can't remember how we got there, but we did.

The prom was quite extravagant. Being that my high school was located in the land of farms and start of suburban sprawl. The majority of students were from farming families and sophistication was not a strong trait among the masses. So to have the prom at a swanky dinner club (remember those) and in a populated suburban area, it was quite special. Most of the dating couples came by motor caravan driven by parents and chaperones. After being dropped off at the entrance, we were escorted to the tables, beautifully decorated with flowers. A program described the menu, evening activities (Welcome, Invocation, even a skit and farewell) letting us know what to expect that evening. We danced to The Buddy Everette Orchestra. No disc jockey. The only disc jockeys known at the time were on the radio. Though I can't remember what they played, I'm sure it was the music of the day. On the table there was also a tiny red-velvet tasseled booklet that served as a keepsake. The theme of the prom was . . .

"Moonlight and Roses 1968"

The march began. Its tempo filtered through the air as the seniors filed in and took their places together for the last time. What exactly is *Pomp & Circumstance*? It is a Triumphal march to a processional tune composed by Sir Edward Elgar on 19 October 1901. Elgar took the phrase "pomp and circumstance" from Shakespeare's "Othello. In Act III, Scene III, the title character refers to the "pride, pomp and circumstance

Farewell the neighing steed and the shrill trump,
The spirit-stirring drum, th'ear-piercing fife,
The royal banner, and all quality,
Pride, pomp, and circumstance of glorious war!

In the United States, the *Trio* section "Land of Hope and Glory" of March No. 1 is often known as "Pomp and Circumstance" or as "The Graduation March" and is played at virtually all high school and some college graduation ceremonies.

Researching the origins of this traditional exercise, I listened to the tune and even after all these years, I can still feel the swell of pride I felt when I marched through that gymnasium with 268 other graduates. Row-by-row we shuffled to our seats to the strains of *Pomp & Circumstance*. I took my place in not quite the last row, to sit through countless boring speeches, accolades, and words of encouragement from the principal, teachers and students.

Then the roll-call began. Because my last name became with "S" I had a long wait before I received my hard-earned diploma. Meanwhile, I joked with those fellow students who sat next to me, however, it was the first time in four years that I had because I was not a popular gal. No matter. We talked, joked and enjoyed the time. What I remember most, other than getting the diploma, was when one of those popular guys asked me why didn't we talked before. Why didn't he get to know me better? I just smiled, and said "Oh well. Too bad, so sad." No, I really didn't say that. It just felt good that he felt sorry and I didn't. I was on to bigger places.

Then I received my diploma.

What Should Be Saved - The Times of Your Life
High School Graduation

My husband, Keith, graduated high school the same year I did. His ceremony lasted much longer since there were 378 graduates in his class. I asked him what he remember. About the same thing I did then recalled when the ceremony was over how all the graduates swung their cap's tassel from the left to the right signifying you graduated. You made it!

When the ceremonies were over, some went to their homes for a big family party and others went out to restaurants. I think much of the same things happen today. Gifts and cards were given to the graduate, ever so thankful when the gift was monetary. Cameras flashed, well-wishes given, food and drinks consumed, and more congratulations offered as everyone went home. Then the grad sat in their room and counted the cash and checks, checked out the gifts, and then it all finally hit home . . . No more school! At least for now or until, and if, the grad went onto college.

When I started to gather my things for the family museum, I was thrilled when I opened a box that had my high school yearbook, diploma (in bad shape because my father had saved it among his greasy tools) and tassel. In Keith's box was his diploma, sports letters and senior picture. All of these precious mementoes' are in our family museum. I also found some cards that somehow got saved. Not only from high school but from Grammar school as well. They are an absolute hoot! Very retro now.

Do you still have your diploma, tassel, yearbook, and cards? If not, I'm sure you wish you had. Perhaps if you do a little searching you may find them. You would be surprised how family members hold onto things, stored in boxes long forgotten. If you ask, they just might say, "Hey sure. I think there are some boxes in the attic/basement that may have some of your things. Let's go get them!" And after you have gathered what remains, please do put them in your museum. If you do not have a family museum, you can arrange your keepsakes in a shadow box that you can hang on your wall. However you display your memories, know that you are preserving your past and giving yourself something to share that many people can relate too. Happy Graduation Day to all.

How to Organize Your Heirlooms:
Find, Select, Display

The key word is organization – one box at a time. It is overwhelming at first, but as they say, *"Rome wasn't built in a day."* Understand that the selecting part takes time. Picking the items out, deciding between one or more of the heirlooms, dividing the space equally, and sometimes having to draw the line as to who gets to put what, where, and how many. Here are two examples of remembrances displayed in our Family Museum.

My husband served in the Naval Reserves for 28 years. He saved many of this uniforms, medals and ribbons, and many pictures. Selecting the best ones, I put together a framed grouping showing the many stages of his Navy career. On another shelf is his collection of navy hats and other keepsakes. He is proud of serving his country and upon retirement he received a large US flag that hangs on the wall in his office instead of being stuffed in a box. It looks really great there!

As careers go, mine was an eclectic one, from fashion model, Kelly Girl, cosmetician, art gallery owner and charity fundraiser, book author and tour guide, I amassed a collection of paper memorabilia showing some of what I accomplished: A poster from an Art Deco exhibit at my gallery, programs from charity events, tour guide flyer, and a copy of each of the books I wrote on colonial history. I achieved much satisfaction from helping others and it does my heart good to see this visual display of my successes.

Another subject for organization is the finding, selecting and displaying of family artwork.

What did you like to draw when you were a kid? From the time a child can pick up a crayon and scribble on paper (maybe on the wall) it is interesting to see. All first scribbles, squiggles and doodles are forms of expression. Ever wonder what is on their little minds while they draw and see the outcome? Are the drawings some kind of clue to the child's future?

For example, this drawing of a train by my husband Keith when he was in first grade, shows his attention to detail. He did not become an engineer, but his love for trains was passed onto his son, Charlie. Though Charlie loved to watch the trains come into the station and he always waved to the engineer when a train passed by, his loved drawing ships. He first drew submarines, then ocean liners. This drawing was found in a Father's Day card Charlie gave to his dad. Charlie did not go on to have a career at sea, but gave him the love of travel and adventure books, and of course, drawing.

How to Organize Your Heirlooms:
Find, Select, Display

The juggler was drawn by our daughter Tiffeni. She would watch her father juggle and this was her interpretation. Her love of expressive art has given her many hours of drawing pleasure and she now passes on her talents to children as a teacher. As for me, the only picture I could find was this drawing of a little girl jumping rope. Self-portrait? Perhaps.

There is so much written on the subject of art that it is truly mind-boggling. But whatever those early images are, they should be saved. And more importantly, to save as much as you can because it is truly amazing to see first-hand how artistic minds are expressed and developed.

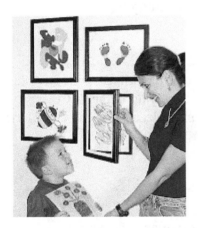

There are many products that you can purchase for the preservation of artwork.

For example these individual frame boxes in which you can both display and store pictures. These units come in various sizes and should be hung on the walls of different rooms, not just the child's bedroom. By displaying their artwork in public areas of the home, the child can feel proud that his family takes much pride in him or her by showing off their artistic talents.

Another storage idea is a multi-drawer cardboard box that stores many papers including school work and school mementoes. When artwork becomes larger in size and multiple in quantity, having a unit like this swinging panel that flips open like a book will present artwork in a movable display.

Whatever presentation method you use, it will give both the artist and the observer hours of pleasure and pride.

We hold onto our possessions because we believe they are important to ourselves, to others, to our family, to our heirs, to our dreams, or to our own personal story. If these items are supposedly so important, the question is <u>how are you treating them?</u> If you value an item, then show it off. Honor the memory by displaying and celebrating the item. The respect you show will result in it having a new meaning and value to you today. Possessions do not mean much when they are stuffed in a drawer or box, but by displaying them, they not only add real value to your life, they properly honor your family's history.

First step – STOP throwing or giving your memories away!

There is much psychology today behind why people save or don't save. We all accumulate things, throw some way, and keep others. We might save for example, our first report cards and love letters. When choosing items you want to put in your family museum, be selective, be discriminating. My basic museum principle is select only what you and your family truly cherish. Identify special mementos. Appreciate quality, not quantity.

Second step – MAKE lists of important times and favorite things.
    Remember, emotions will influence your choices. Celebrations, accomplishments, occasions, people, places visited, etc. Under each category, list, for example:

Personal celebrations:
    Birthday, anniversary, graduations
Accomplishments:
    Awards, trophies, certificates of achievement
Occasions:
    Holiday presents, special outfit or costume
People:
    Photographs of relatives & friends, school yearbooks
Places visited:
    Family vacations & reunions, class trips

Third step – RECALL if and what you saved & where they may be now. Who may have kept them over the years? Everyone saves things, not only theirs but yours, too. Check in with the grandparents, aunts and uncles, brothers and sisters, and friends.

Fourth step – FINDING space can be a challenge.
But don't despair! There are many options to display and store your family's cherished possessions. The main objective is to create a place for all family members to enjoy.

Fifth step – CREATING your museum is a cooperative venture.
Assembling various items is an artistic endeavor. The arranging is enterprising and every earnest attempt and cooperation needs consideration. Gather a diversified assortment from:

Various people:
>   Yourself, family and friends

Places lived & visited:
>   To form a wide spectrum of history

Select and mix things:
>   Remember *variety is the spice of life*

Your museum is a healthy way to build family closeness in the present and for the future. Perhaps you ask, why cling to the past? I prefer *embrace*. Emotional attachment is not a bad thing. Your museum highlights your family's beliefs, traditions and life stages. It is good and wise to retain as many of your recollections as possible, especially if and when you can no longer see or give a hug to that person. So hold on to the memories.

"Keep some souvenirs of your past, or how will you ever prove it wasn't all a dream?"
~ Ashleigh Brilliant

There is an art to display. Look at museum's smaller collections, department store windows or visit antique shops and observe how a vendor presents their collections. The space you have will dictate how you will display your heirlooms. Organize items in groups. The main idea is to express through display the history of the heirloom and the person, place and event behind it. You want to invite your guests to look closely at your collections, to touch them, encouraging them to ask questions so you can tell your stories and they can tell you theirs.

Now you ask, where is there space in my home? Take a walk around your house, apartment, condo, wherever you call home. Pay particular attention to unused space. Closets, spare bedrooms, roomy hallways. A modicum of space in the living, dining, and family room will do fine. Assess the space. What is there now? How is it used? What is displayed? Can it be moved somewhere else? Can you eliminate some of those things?

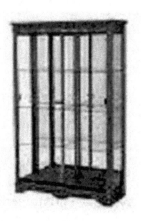

Bookcases, china and curio cabinets can be mini-museums. Even create personal museums, such as in the home office displaying the occupant's career. Also in a child's bedroom where they can create their own museum.

For instance, clothing. My husband saved all of his naval uniforms. Why? It's not as if he was going to mop the deck anytime in the future. So out of his collection, he picked his navy hats and the photograph of when he made Chief Petty Officer. The rest was passed down to family members and donated to our local theater group.

When it came to my Barbie dolls, I wanted all of them in the museum. Also, the kitchen set and dress case. Oh, woe was me to have to select. But I did and got it all in and still had room for more. And when I find a Barbie item I didn't have but always wanted, I get it and add it to my collection.

Use a <u>Chest of Drawers</u> from which small pieces of clothing can be hung from the handles. Larger pieces, such as a suit or gown can be laid in an open drawer. Other items can be stored in closed drawers, preserving and protecting them for perhaps use in the future or when an opportunity comes your way and you want to wear it once again. What fun it is to wear vintage clothing.

<u>Curio cabinets</u> are great places to display small pieces such as jewelry boxes, antique books, and hand-made pieces.

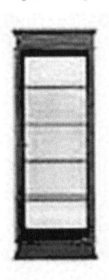

<u>Regard rugs and carpets</u> like a tapestry and hang it on a wall. Use a gallery light to enhance the image or pattern.

Deciding, sorting, keeping, discarding, displaying and storing items in your Family Museum may seem like a daunting task, and sometimes it is. I have been perplexed, uncertain, frustrated, bemused and amused. And I needed help. I told the family that this endeavor is for everyone and that we all need to be involved with the making of our museum.

There is also the "art of rearrangement." As time goes on and items get added to the museum or taken or stored away, reorganization occurs and this is a good thing. It is a way to once again be creative with your displays while continuing to preserve and protect your memories.

When everyone works together, not only does it make the process easier, it makes it fun. So, do not be overwhelmed. Take your time, be patient, think about each item you place on the shelf, on the wall, in the drawer, or even back in the box. You can display it later and when the time comes to pass it on, it is already packed and ready to go.

"Coming together is a beginning. Keeping together is progress.
Working together is success." ~ *Henry Ford*

*"Too many Americans have ignored their
ancestors and family history
and not bothered to examine their own life
stories, much less share them with others.
They too rarely share much of their past lives
with friends, or pass them on to their progeny.
And yet we desperately need to do all that."*

~ Ashleigh Brilliant
Author & Syndicated Cartoonist

Be a Curator – Part One
Deciding, Sorting, Keeping, Displaying and Storing

When going through the boxes and plastic containers, ask yourself what should you keep? What should you release? Where will your treasurers ultimately reside? As you do, be thoughtful and look at what was saved with new eyes. Do the items still please you, intrigue you, teach you about a subject that continues to hold fascination for you? For your family? For the next generation? *Yes!*

Questions for keeping	**Reasons for saving**
- Why am I keeping this	- Because I want to
- Where to keep it	- Create a Family Museum
- Something I really want	- Did and still do
- Can it still be used	- Probably not, but that's ok
- Is it still attractive	- Beauty is in the eye of the beholder
- Is it still functional	- Possibly, but not necessary
- Is it obsolete	- Could be but no matter
- Is it damaged	- Yes/No. No matter
- Should it get fixed	- Maybe, but no need to
- Does keeping it matter	- Absolutely
- Does it have value	- Yes! It's priceless

Ask yourself how you would feel if it isn't in your world any longer? *It depends on how important it is.*

Who would care if you got rid of it? *Your family.* Does it really matter? *Yes!*

What's the worst thing that could happen if you let it go? *Never have it again.*

Do you feel buried in treasurers? *Ask how you would feel if you didn't keep those treasures.*

Do you think you are a prisoner of your possessions? *Think instead yourself as a Caretaker.*

Be a Curator – Part Two
Deciding, Sorting, Keeping, Displaying and Storing Items in Your Museum

A museum archive stores artifacts that may have been excavated from sites like in Egypt. Then the museum curator decides what to display. Your objects may have come from more humble places such as the basement, garage, closet, shed or storage unit, but these are no less places of wonder, but now you are the museum curator, selecting the pieces to display in your home, or places of business, creating a wonderful place filled with a heirlooms and artifacts for all to enjoy today, tomorrow and generations from now. Here are examples of how to and where to display your treasures.

Art Collections: thought provoking memories
Set aside time to go through your family's art works together.

Assess the wall and counter space in your museum area or other room.

Install shelving made for framed and flat artwork. This storage can be placed in a closet or free-standing cabinet.

When the artwork is that of a child's, be circumspect.

Save the best and put the others in a labeled folder to file. Create an online photo album or notebook

album with clear pocket sleeves to display, protect and save the artwork. If the child's precious artwork is not on display in the museum, ensure them that their art is kept safe in the archives.

This is an excellent time to create a household inventory and record it in an inventory book. There is a section for photographs with a page for listing all the information about the piece; what it is, including style and period, date purchased and price and current value if you have the piece appraised. You can also create this document on your computer and save it there or on disc. Photograph digitally or create a special album to display and record the art objects rendered to storage before you choose to give it away or sell it, find another home for the treasure, but most of all, before you think of throwing it away! Physical inventories are important to have, particularly for insurance coverage. In case of any disaster causing the loss of your possessions, you now have proof of their existence and the value therein. History as taught us that if it were not for the physical inventories taken by households from the past, diligently logged into and recorded in both small and large books for posterity, how would our descendants know what they had. They wouldn't.

Photos and photo albums: a daunting task

Sort through, keep the best shots, dispose ruined or duplicate photos.
Replace albums if they are in poor condition. Create new ones with archival materials.

Frame and place photos in the museum to enhance the history of the displayed object.

Copy and save digitally. The satisfaction from preserving those moments-in-time will be gratifying.

Oral history: Stories, conversations, music

Voices are precious. How many times were there when you could tell who was in the room by simply listening to their voice?

Before you start recording, gently prepare the person by giving them the opportunity to talk about what they want to talk about. Encourage them to laugh, even sing. And if and when the tone changes, seize it.

Here is an idea for perpetuity. Have the person select something from your Family Museum that they remember and have them tell a story about it.

How I wish I would have done the same with many of the heirlooms in our Grandparent's Museum. All I can do now is tell their story in my words, with my voice.

Capturing indelible memories

Endearing images on film. If your family is like mine, we have rolls and rolls of film, many unidentifiable because someone failed to write on the box what was filmed. These moments are just as precious as voice recordings because you can see who, what, where, when and why the film was made. Keep the solid film format and back it up on disc and on a hard drive. And with today's technology, a short film clip can be made an inserted into a small device that can be kept in the museum. This would enhance the perspective memory.

Be a Curator – Part Two
Deciding, Sorting, Keeping, Displaying and Storing Items in Your Museum

The written Word: Engaging reflections

Letters, diaries, journals, bibles, documents, even wills, tell stories of the lives and times of the writer. When I found letters my mother wrote to my father while he was in the navy during WWII, it was like reading a history book. She wrote what was going on in her city, what movies she saw, about volunteering at the USO, and much more. She was not very political but she wrote about listening to President Roosevelt, food rationing, and her family. I do not know what happened to the letters my father wrote back to her, but there were little clues within her letters that told of a love that was unsure. There is a wealth of wonderful stories in old letters that should be saved and cherished.

The need for transcription

Whether letters were written in longhand or on early typewriters, they may be hard to read. Some letters can be scanned and saved to disc. Some may even need to be transcribed, especially if they were written in a foreign language. My father kept some letters from relatives in Lithuania who could only write in their language. I was fortunate enough to find someone who could translate them and painstakingly typed them anew. Then there was a Thanksgiving dinner with the relatives to whom these letters were about and it was a joy to hear them read them. If you do not save these documents and transcribe/translate what you can, you may never see and hear their words again.

Archives: Your personal library

Like encyclopedia's, the archives you create are for and about your family's heritage, culture and the diversity therein. Archives are places where your history is ripe for rediscovery. Preserving paper takes special care. Why? If an acidic product comes into contact with paper, photos, textiles or other similar items, the acid can migrate, causing permanent damage and decay. This is why it is important to use good quality Acid-Free and archival materials for the preservation of your treasured memories.

Just as recording and preserving formats change, so is our world ever-changing. Archivists are strong believers in *'better safe than sorry'*, so endeavor and make every effort and attempt to save your family history.

Memory . . . is the diary that we all carry about with us."
~ Oscar Wilde

Building your Family Museum does not have to feel like a monumental task. Having a plan and preparing the steps, like setting up the ingredients for a recipe, will help you immensely. The most important factor that will determine what tools you will need is what style and the location of the museum you want to build.

Depending on whether you use freestanding furniture, ready-made cabinetry, install do-it-yourself modular units, or hire a carpenter to build a custom unit, give yourself and the carpenter plenty of time to create your museum. Work together to select what type of wood, finish, paint color, trim, accessories, lighting, glass doors and/or shelves will be best for your museum. Identify the size and content of your heirlooms and explore your museum style options and location/s. Before you decide, do a little research before selecting and shopping. There is a plethora of resources to visit either by searching the Internet or by going to the brick-and-mortar stores to find, learn and compare all the things you need to construct your museum.

Solid Hardwoods

Light-toned woods: oak, ash, maple, beech, and birch. Dark-toned species: cherry, walnut, and mahogany. Budget-minded hardwoods: alder, poplar, and aspen. Softwoods: pine, fir, and knotty pine. Wood boards come in many lengths & widths and can be stained or painted. Carpentry skills are necessary to fashion these woods into the sizes you need.

Sheet Products

Hardwood-veneered plywood can be used for constructing your museum. Plywood panels are more stable than solid lumber and less likely to warp. Plywood used for shelving is usually surfaced on front and back with attractive hardwood veneers such as oak, maple, ash or cherry. It comes in various qualities or grades, depending on if the wood will be stained or painted. In shelf construction, the plywood is usually edged with hardwood veneer tape or trimmed with solid hardwood.

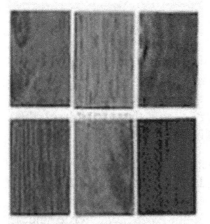

Plastic Laminates:

Durable and easy to clean, laminates are popular materials for shelving. Keep in mind they are made of particleboard and the least durable product. A grade up is melamine because of the layer of special paper saturated with a melamine resin. Both affordable and come in many colors. Shelf Kits are vinyl-wrapped shelves, easy to assemble and are inexpensive. Readily available at all building material stores.

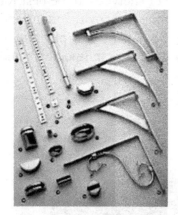

Shelf Hardware:

To support the undersides of shelves, tracks and brackets, the adjustable hardware comes in a variety of finishes and lengths. Pine Gusset brackets are attractive but less flexible. Make sure that this hardware is firmly secured into the walls because as the weight of the artifacts increase, you want to make sure the shelf will never collapse, which could cause an unpleasant situation.

Glass Shelving:

Used in freestanding pieces of furniture such as china and curio cabinets, plate glass is a popular shelf material for displays because it allows you to view objects more fully and does not block the light. Tempered safety glass is the best. There are different edge types available:

Seamed Edge:

After the shelf is cut, the edges are sanded to dull the sharp edges. This is to make the glass shelf is safe to handle.

Flat Polish Edge: the edges of the glass shelf have been polished to a smooth shiny finish.

Pencil Polish Edge: Popular with circle or oval shapes, the side edge is rounded for a softer look.

Beveled Polish Edge: edges of the glass shelf are cut and polished in an angle with a specific Bevel Width to produce a certain "look". This process leaves the glass shelf thinner around the edges and thicker in the center. The Bevel Width around the glass shelf can range in size from 1/4" to 1 3/4" and is specified by you.

Lighting

Proper museum lighting is vital whether using wall systems, freestanding furniture, shelving, shadow boxes or a coffee table. When lighting is installed, make sure it fits the needs of the display. Installing lighting during the construction may require the services of an electrician. And make sure there is ventilation. Lights heat up small spaces fast and a cool stable temperature needs to be maintained at all times. Locate lights at the top of the unit or ceiling-mounted on tracks with the light directed down on the unit. Swivel track lighting aimed at a unit, highlighting any display, including shadow boxes.

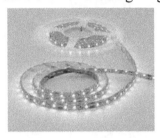

Concealed Strip lights (rope lights) housed on a flexible backing strip is tucked inside clear or colored plastic tubing. Halogen, incandescent, fluorescent and gallery lights, wall sconces, small lamps, and other discreet fixtures, whatever you choose, you should not see the bulbs, just the glow. Always keep ventilation in mind and a dimmer switch is a big plus for any lighting scheme. With proper lighting, *Your Family Museum* will be aesthetically pleasing and inspiring.

Finishing Touches

Stained or painted shelves, wallpaper or painted walls, give a finished look. Create storage below the bottom shelf and conceal with a door(s) or drapery material. Use small easels, plate hangers and picture frames to enhance the display. Use Styrofoam blocks and step shelves to build height adding space and dimension to the display. To secure and support the items use proper size nails, staples, glue, thumbtacks, Velcro strips and tabs, picture hooks, and museum gel. You will finding most of what you need at arts & craft stores. Details make a difference.

Visit museums and antique shops. Observe how the artifacts are displayed. Pay attention to the color and patterns on the walls, how textured materials create interesting backdrops and how acrylic, metal or wood easels incorporate height and support.

Whatever space you use for *Your Family Museum*, you want to clearly showcase all of the heirlooms, artifacts, books, pictures, etc., highlighting your family's history. And be creative. Try different setups and themes. Do not be afraid to change, add or subtract things. When something else is found, put it in the museum. If things get piled on top one another and space is no longer available, re-arrange. It takes a bit of time, but it is a good thing to re-acquaint yourself with what is in the museum. No matter why or how often you spend time in the Family Museum, have fun!

Create with the heart; build with the mind." ~ Criss Jami, Artist

Where to Locate Your Family Museum

Walk around your house, apartment, condo, wherever you call home. Go room-by-room paying close attention to unused space. But you see no space, just lack of space. Every wall and corner is occupied by something. This is where your fine eye is needed; assess what is there now. How is it used? If something is displayed there, what is it? Can it be moved to another room? Can you eliminate it? Consider replacing a piece of furniture with a different piece, such as a bookcase or curio cabinet that can showcase your heirlooms. They make excellent mini-museums. Even create personal museums, such as in the home office displaying the occupant's career. Also in a child's bedroom where they can create their own museum.

The Living room is sometimes the loneliest room in the house, besides perhaps the dining room. You walk through them, maybe take a book and sit down for a while because it's quiet in there. Maybe instead of eating in the kitchen you take your cup of coffee and sit at the dining room table, recalling or planning a family feast. But here are rooms that really lend them self as locations for your Family Museum.

Family rooms, or as they are called today - 'great rooms' - serve many purposes. This room can also be a wonderful place to display family memorabilia. Either a custom-built unit designed around the big screen TV where you can safely display precious items behind glass doors or behind solid doors for storage.

Hallways are often overlooked as a place for a Family Museum. Many are narrow and doors take up wall space. Traffic fills up these places. People, pets and other assorted perambulators run amuck up and down these passages. But there are a number of ways you can employ to create a display space by using ledges.

The Master Bedroom is a good place to display personal items and collections that would not necessarily fit a family museum. This room should evoke an area of peace and calm and tranquility. No need for foot traffic and congestion. Visitors are welcome upon invitation.

Children's Bedrooms should definitely have space for keepsakes and collections. Children need to see their interests and accomplishments displayed for their well-being as well as to share with friends and family.

A Guest Bedroom is an ideal place for a Family Museum. Depending on how often it is used, the serenity and space to display family heirlooms offers your guests the opportunity to get to know your family better.

Home offices and offices away from home are ideal places to showcase the occupant's career. Big desks and maybe disorganized bookshelves tend to contribute to distraction instead of appreciating the pursuits it took to achieve the success held in this room. It's time to show off those skills and achievements.

Closets are the perfect place, but also the most challenging since they are usually stuffed to the gills with clothes, shoes, linens, even suitcases. There are a few ways that can provide storage space, for example, employing a wonderful antique armoire or even a cabinet that usually has a television in it, and with the aid of a tension rod, clothes can be hung and with the ease of the pullout drawer, small linens or items of clothing can be stored there. Once the closet is cleared out, replace wire shelves with wood or glass shelfs, make sure the lighting is sufficient, which can also provide indirect night-light, and install a French Doors to show off what is inside.

Following are images of ways and means to give you the big picture on these multiple locations. No matter where or how you create the Family Museum, be proud of it. Show it off. Talk about it. Encourage others to do the same and mostly, enjoy it!   *"Every cubic inch of space is a miracle."*   ~ *Walt Whitman*

What a lovely room. Time ago this room was called the Front Parlor and reserved for special guests and occasions. Some houses today do not have living rooms. And how many times a day do you just walk through it or by it? Most likely the room is used for visiting or where the Christmas tree is place. By putting your Family Museum here, this room will have distinction. But how? By using a coffee table.

Using this table is an ingenious way to make the humdrum coffee table become a truly interesting piece of furniture in your home. Most of these tables are large and though they perform a functional use and place to put inanimate objects upon, the coffee table can be so much more.

It can become your Family Museum.

Coffee tables come in a variety of sizes and styles, as seen here by some photos culled from online images. You can find them in furniture stores, antique shops and on the Internet. But if you have particular requirements for the objects you want to display, have it custom-made to your specifications.

When designing this type of display unit, consider incorporating a sliding tray, allowing you to slip it in and out with ease when placing on the heirlooms or collections. This ability will keep the table top clear for anything you place there. Lighting and ventilation are important elements to factor into the design.

This type of Family Museum allows you to change, add to, or remove objects from the display. Keep in mind the size and height of the artifacts. You may want to concentrate on heirlooms from one family member or a combination of several pieces of memorabilia that make up an interesting story about the owner(s) of the artifacts.

In my family's living room there is a *Chickering* Piano my mother purchased after she was married. Many a family gathering brought out my two uncles; one on the piano, the other singing, bringing the house down every time. My mother played well enough, not reading sheet music but playing 'by ear." My brother took piano lessons and was good enough to make an appearance at a piano recital in Chicago. When we moved to the country, the piano moved with us, followed by several more moves, finally coming to rest in my home.

Ever since I could remember, there were always two figurines on the top of the piano and a print of an Italian garden. To this day, the picture is still the same but the figurines changes. Now there are two of my favorite statues; a Colonial Man & Woman, coyly flirting with each other. On the man's base is the signature of *Carlo Mollica*. It took me a while to research the name, but when I found it, the information said the figurines were made by one of the oldest and most collectible of ceramics factories in Italy.

The Mollica factory began in 1880 in Naples. It moved to Milan in 1942. Between 1950 and 1970 the factory reached its zenith of popularity under the leadership of Carlo Mollica. During this period Mollica produced artwork equal to the finest made throughout Italy. The factory produced a wide range of products from classical Capodimonte to Lenci-like Art Nouveau. Mollica ceased operation in 1978. Walter Del Pellegrino, author of Italian Pottery Marks from Cantagalli to Fornasetti, 1850-1950.

In conclusion, the Living Room is an excellent location to display your collections, being in a coffee table or on top of a piano. It is a pleasure to sit awhile and gaze upon the lovely things you collect. There is something comforting about surrounding yourself or gathering with family heirlooms in the Living Room.

How many times when you were a child did you hear, "Don't touch that!" or, "Be extra careful when you dust that!" or this one, "Don't run through the house. Certain things could fall and you will be in a lot of trouble if they do!"

Vases on the hall table, plates hanging on the wall, statues on the piano, fancy candy dish on the coffee table. I grew up with these things as many of you have, too. Some were passed down to me, others I collected myself. Do you have pieces of fine china, porcelain and glass in your home? I like displaying these items, therefore, I do not have them in my family museum. And as I dust them for the millionth time (maybe not quite that many) I can still hear, "Be careful with that vase. It was your grandmother's. It proudly sat on the dining room table for years. When she passed away, my mother took possession of it. She proudly displayed it in the living room. As a child I never sought to know anything about it except that it was old and pretty. Then one day, it almost met its demise when it fell, ending up in big and small chunks strewed about the room. I can still remember watching my dad sitting at the kitchen table, painstakingly gluing the vase back together. Now I have it and the vase still reigns supreme, high on top the dining room china cabinet, bruised but still beautiful.

The important thing about collecting china and porcelain is to first, cherish the ones you have, not only when they are on display, but in a preservation mode with pictures and written documentation. Analysis the characteristics of the piece, the material of which it is made, how the image is put on the piece, and importantly, its mark on the bottom. Some pieces may not have one, but that does not mean it is of lesser value. But for serious collectors, those marks are extremely important. To assist you in determining those marks, go online to find guides to antique pottery marks, porcelain marks and china marks. An example of a china mark is this one: Nippon China.

Nippon era began in 1891 when the Japanese porcelain was clearly marked "Nippon" due to the McKinley Tariff Act. This act required that all porcelain be marked with the country of origin. ("Nippon" literally translates to "Japan".) This porcelain was made specifically to be exported to the west with designs and patterns that suited Americans tastes. At that time, Japan had a thriving porcelain industry using methods used in Europe and the United States. The Japanese items were less expensive than pieces coming from Europe and became very popular in the U.S. The porcelain was sold in gift shops, dime stores, fairs and even at the local grocery. Nippon items were also sold by Montgomery Ward, Sears & Roebuck, mail order houses and other department stores. In 1921 the United States government changed its position and required that Japanese imports no longer be marked "Nippon," but with, "Japan." This marks the end of the Nippon era.

The Dining Room

How many of you grew up with a Dining room in your house? This was by far one of the most important rooms because it was where the family gathered for special occasions. Sadly, this room as been reviewed as an unnecessary room by today's needs. No longer do families gather around a commodious table and share a special meal. They now choose to eat in a kitchen or family room, using TV trays or other tables. Perhaps one day the Dining Room will regain its importance in the home as well as in the customary practices of family gatherings.

In my family's dining room there is a buffet, hutch, table and chairs inherited from my Italian Grandmother. As the story goes, she had purchased this entire suite from Sears Roebuck in 1920. It could have been via the mail-order catalog or directly from the store since she lived in Chicago. At this time there was a colonial-revival period of which was this extraordinary rich mahogany set was inspired. Six chairs with Chippendale backs, table with built-in extension leaf underneath, buffet with plenty of storage and china cabinet with Chippendale-pane windows was really something in its time. When she passed away, the furniture traveled among family member and eventually came to me. I had all the pieces restored and feel very proud to have her furniture in my home.

English Bone China with its castle motif was very popular. These dishes were used for special occasions only. Perhaps that is why I still have them. My mother inherited the dishes and passed them down to me. I am thrilled to keep the furniture and dishes together.

In the dining room is a white Bisque Compote Dish with three cherubs and two candlesticks each with a cherub. Circa 1965? This piece gives me the heebie-jeebies every time I pick it up to move it. So it has been sitting on the small silverware chest instead of on the table for years. But in order to get to the silverware in the top drawer, I have to pick up the compote. Oh dear me!

In conclusion, Dining Rooms are a good location for your collections. They say a lot about you and your home. Always surround you and your family with as much beauty as you can.

In many houses there are spaces devoted to entertainment called Media Rooms. When I was a kid, there were no "Family Rooms." Rooms like these were down in the finished basement and called Rumpus (noisy disturbance) Rooms where the kids played games, watched TV shows and listen to music. Commonly, the television (separate from the stero/hi-fi player) was in the living room. The family pretty much watched the same TV shows because there were only three to five major broadcasting stations: ABC, NBC, and CBS. Bigger cities had their own stations. Where I grew up, we had WGN.

Today, big screen TVs dominate the center of the room, some situated in large cabinets with shelves, fixed to a wall or freestanding. Some screens are set over fireplaces, framed by bookshelves. These shelves hold not only books; they are filled with bric-a-brac (small ornamental objects of interest or sentimental value). Now here is a great place to devote to the Family Museum.

First, take off all the things that are irrelevant. Distribute unrelated items elsewhere in your home. By relocating things, they become important again.

Envision what you want to show case, which will depend on the size and amount of shelf space there is. One way to display many items is by creating mini-museums incorporated in shadow boxes (more on this later). By putting together photograph and keepsakes, you create a story about a relative, special event, precious artifacts, etc. The shadow boxes also keep things dust-free and safe. This method will also allow you to move the display easily.

By changing a media center bookcase into a family museum with heirlooms, there is much more to look at and appreciate. And when you watch TV and become bored with the show, you can turn the TV off and let your eyes wonder and focus on the family collections and maybe drift off into a different place and time. What fun!

The Family Room is also a great place to have a coffee table museum as well. Being that this room is a gathering place for all sorts of activity, just like a coffee table in the living room, when guests and family members take their seat on the sofa, they can peer down into the table and gaze upon a thoughtfully assembled display of family artifacts. When they want to look closer at an item, you can simply pull open the drawer, take the item(s) out and put them back. What an imaginative way to adapt a means to and end and to engage the humble coffee table for a new use and purpose - Your Family Museum.

Whatever good things we build end up building us.
~ Jim Rohn, Architect

The Hallway Shadow Boxes

Here's a step-by-step guide on how to create a shadow box:

1. Focal point: object you want to draw attention to (your centerpiece).

    ·   A memento, souvenir, keepsake, artifact, historical object

    ·   A collection item from a hobby (pursuit/ pastime) or study

    ·   A photograph, letter, newspaper headline, postcard, art image

    ·   A artistic rendering (painting, drawing, needlework, sculpture)

2. Background: shadowbox backer (usually included) or your choice.

    ·   Scrapbook paper, gift-wrapping paper, wallpaper samples

    ·   Fabric, clothing remnant such as an image from a t-shirt

    ·   Paper such as maps, newspaper, and sheet music (found at antique stores)

3. Attaching items: decide whether you want a permanent or temporary fix. Try:

    ·   Pins or Photo corners, double-sided removable scrapbooking tape

    ·   Double-stick foam mounting tape, Velcro hook-and-loop tape

    ·   Hot and/or craft glue, Photo Mount acid-free adhesive

    ·   Magnets with foam adhesive (many sizes)

4. Details: add items to accent the focal point

    ·   Photos of a special moment that gives emphasis to

    ·   Found objects that highlight the focal point

    ·   Ribbon, flowers, or buttons that accent the treasure

    ·   Use an alphabetical letter to make a word, name or date that draws attention

5. Be creative: There are many ingenious ways to use and display shadowbox(s).

As the hallway serves as passageway, floor space is not an option. But the walls can provide the space you need by incorporating ledges. And if there is an area for a chair or two, what a delightful place to take a moment to sit and rest and gaze upon the artifacts belonging to your family. A mere glance of a memory is quite satisfying as you go through your day.

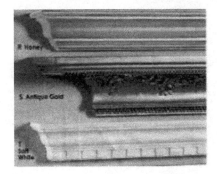

Display ledges come in a variety sizes and materials, such as solid hardwoods and light weight high-density resins. Two depths are available and they have raised edges, keeping items from falling off. Some have plate groves. Other styles are corner and quilt rack shelves.

Torison boxes (floating) shelves are fixed and have no visible hardware to mar clean lines for a modern look. Ledges can be arranged in virtually any pattern on a wall and need to be anchored into the wall studs for sufficient support. As you arrange the items on the ledges be cognitive of subject matter and sizes of objects. Place the ledges high enough for comfortable viewing and so nobody conks their head on it or flying arms and hands don't knock the precious heirlooms off. View ledge manufacturer websites to get layout & arrangement ideas.

Hallway lighting is paramount for successful display. Track lighting is fine but make sure it is not over powering. Sconces and picture gallery lights work well also. Whichever way you fashion your collections using the hallway or hall walls, you will be surprised at how much space there is to display memorabilia. Now this area can be called the Hallway Family Museum.

What a great way to preserve family history! Shadow Boxes are vignettes of a concise reminiscent account, description, or episode, evoking images, memories and feelings. With a few artifacts belonging to an ancestor you can tell a lovely anecdote focusing on a time in their life.

Manufacturers of shadow boxes can be purchased online or in craft stores, offering many sizes, styles, finishes, glass and lighting. Request a lock and key if needed. The boxes can also be made-to-order. The content will dictate the size.

When arranging the items, be mindful of the thickness of the objects. For example, this Mardi Gras porcelain mask is rounded, therefore, the box needed to be deep. You do not want the boxes to be so deep they protrude from the wall, especially in a hallway. If one is needed, a carpenter can install the shadow box into the wall. This would also be an opportunity to install electrical connection for lighted boxes.

This shadow box exhibits miscellaneous pieces of jewelry I have collected over the years. I can recall exactly when I received the piece which allows me to visit my past and appreciate the reason why I received it, such as the blue ballerina pin. I saw this at a grade school Christmas bazaar and told my mom I just had to have it. One day when I went back to see it again, it was gone and felt so sad. Then on Christmas

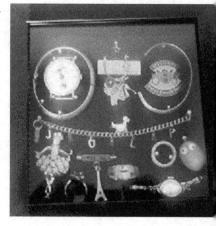

morning, there it was, tucked inside a small jewelry box. I wore that pin to school every day. I always wanted to be a ballerina, but alas, that dream didn't come true. But I still have the pin and the fond memory that goes with it. Thanks Mom!

When arranging several shadow boxes, do them the same way when grouping photographs. Be attentive to size, the horizontal and vertical structures of the boxes, and the dimensions – length, width, height – before hanging them on the wall. If there are several boxes telling a story, arrange them in a comprehensible manner so the observer will understand the story you are telling.

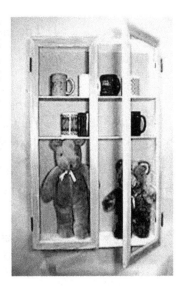

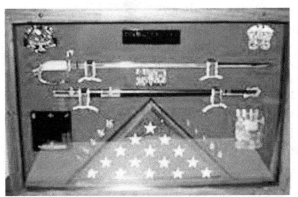

Be circumspect when creating the shadow box. You want to capture the essence of the person's character.

Selecting the choicest and most essential artifacts and photographs of the ancestor will result in honoring that special person and time. What satisfaction you will have as well as a great feeling pride for preserving the family heirlooms in a Shadow Box Family Museum.

The Guest Bedroom
Curio Cabinets

The empty bedroom; or whatever reason the room is not occupied, then why not occupy it with your Family Museum. There are several ways you can accomplish this. The rooms' purpose, usefulness and size will be your guide when choosing a curio cabinet(s) to display the heirlooms. They can be petite or grand. They can go in the corner of a room or by using several cabinets, they can take up a whole wall. Yet, as small as some curio cabinets can be, they are nevertheless a great place to showcase the family heirlooms.

There are several styles of cabinets available at furniture stores and online. One can also be custom-built to meet your requirements based on the objects to be displayed. Most curio cabinets come with lighting, glass shelves and beveled glass doors.

One challenge about glass shelves is some may not be provided with a groove to support dishes. This is easily remedied by using clear museum gel, a clear removable adhesive that secures not only dishes but also any object that may be vulnerable to falling. Also purchase small plate stands. Bookends are good for all support needs. For a thoughtful touch, place a photograph of the person to whom the heirloom belonged to which defines and associates the item with the person and adds more interest.

Once your curio cabinet is filled and you show your guests the objects displayed there, refer to the cabinet as the *Family Museum*. That always sparks their interest. You can even apply a small brass plaque identifying the museum. For example, *Collection of Grandmother's China Dolls.*

After your museum is completed, what a pleasure it will be when you walk into that bedroom and no longer feel loneliness there. And what a delight it will be for your guests. The museum will be a great way to introduce them to your family and encourage conversations. You may even inspire them to create their own.

For more ideas, visit a museum. Take a look at the smaller exhibits of artifacts displayed. Due to the massive security museums employ, these diminutive collections are sealed in glass-enclosed chambers. Not much different from a curio cabinet except, of course, you cannot open the glass doors and take the heirloom out anytime you please.

However, you can in your museum. Antique shops do an admirable job displaying a plethora of items. These displays will show you how unrelated items can work together.

Be creative. Have fun.

Bedrooms come in all sizes and shapes. Some are merely sufficient for sleeping, with closets that can take up a lot of room. Then there are those bedrooms that come with small seating areas devoted to a little haven of peace. Some bedrooms also have a separate room for clothing storage and even space for dressing. That is nice, but not in an average home. But whatever the dimensions and free floor space is available, somewhere there is, even if it is a small portion of the room, space for a little museum. Consider putting a curio cabinet or decorative shelf to display cherished keepsakes.

For example, I have a miniature book and perfume bottle collection that I have gathered over the years. The books are displayed in an antique lady's desk and share space with miscellaneous gifts and knick-knacks.

This picture does not show the collection of miniature perfume bottles, however, I set them up to take this picture to show them. As I did, I opened each tiny bottle and was delighted to whiff the fragrance that was still lingering inside the bottle, triggering many a memory.

Another collection near and dear to the family are the porcelain *Lladros*. Over the years many were given as tokens of love and for special occasions. Years ago my husband and I were fortunate to travel to Madrid, Spain and visit several Lladro Galleries. We were amazed at the variety and size of statues available for sale. These artistic creations take your breath away.

We have stopped collecting Lladro's, so what we have is cherished all the more. Collections of one type of item do not belong in a Family Museum because they do not tell of a particular history or event shared by the family, therefore, by locating them in their own setting, the items have their own special presence, to be appreciated just as they are.

The Child(ren's) Bedroom(s)
Many Ideas

There is nothing more satisfying then when a parent goes into a child's bedroom and can see the floor. Trying to keep their room orderly is a monumental task. Trying to instill the merit of a neat room is just as difficult. There really is not a sure way to get them to do either. But one thing you can get kids to do is to show off their hobbies, collections and interests. A great way to do this is by having them create their own museum.

If closet space is not an option, here are several creative ways.

First, ask your child how he or she envisions their museum. Get them involved and the whole family will have fun.

Factory-made mullion glass-fronted wall cabinets with solid or glass shelves, such as those found in a kitchen, is an option to consider when planning built-in display and storage for the child's room.

There are three configurations: base, wall, and specialty cabinets. For the bedroom, wall cabinets are the best. You can place them side-by-side and stack them to create all sizes of family museums.

Wall space will dictate how many cabinets you can use.

Ceiling height determines how high to place the cabinets, but do not put it up to the ceiling.

Make sure the lighting in the cabinets are ventilated. If you cannot do the job yourself, where you purchase the cabinets, they can recommend a carpenter.

Bedroom furniture can now be pushed up against the wall making floor space available. Sold through cabinet dealers and home-improvement centers, manufactured cabinets come in many styles. Do not use every wall. Save space for bulletin and art boards.

The Child(ren's) Bedroom(s)
Many Ideas

Another area to display large objects, like model boats that can take up a lot of space, is by putting them on the top of a window valance. Not only does this put them in a regal realm, it keeps them out of harm's way. A valance also is great at concealing the top of draperies, curtains, and window shades. By constructing a wooden valance (a trim carpenter can scallop the edge for a more decorative look) with a solid top, is a perfect place for displays. For example, my son has a collection of large ship models, even a three-foot long Titanic. There is also The Queen Mary I & II, and aircraft carrier USS Independence.

Dormer windows are under-estimated. Though it usually is a place for a window seat, this is really a great place to showcase a particular item or items. The space below can be used for storage. If the dormer space is large and accommodates more than one window, the space can be separated in sections, devoting perhaps a collection of dolls and furniture, dollhouses, large toys like rocking horses, baby dolls with their prams, etc., into their own display. This area can also be enhanced with low-watt lighting. If you install glass doors, remember ventilation.

Once your child/children organize their keepsakes, they will have a great time displaying and showing their collections to friends & family. Their museum identifies them, their accomplishments, instills pride and contributes to the building of a future viable resume.

*"Not only should we encourage kids to daydream,
but also to jump-in and build those dreams."*
~ Ryan Lilly

97

More than ever, today's workplaces are at home. What a great place for a *Personal Museum of Success,* dedicated to the occupants' career or profession.

The type of occupation will determine the space needed to accommodate collected memorabilia showcasing the stages of a career such as tools-of-trade, books, and military items for service to our country.

For example, after my husband retired from the Navy, he was presented with a large American Flag. He did not want to keep it folded up and in the display box, so he hung it on the wall. His Certificate of Honorable Discharge hangs above his desk.

Other items such as photographs, licenses, framed certificates(s), letters of acknowledgment, books, trophies and keepsakes from past jobs and careers add stories and memories that led to his success.

In my home office, one can tell it is a writer's domain, filled with books and all sorts of knick-knacks. It is also the home of a quirky collection of Mexican Feather Art. My collection started with my mother's purchase she made

when she went to Mexico with her sister on her honeymoon in 1945. She passed it onto me after I married. Since then I collected many more and always on the lookout for others. I hope I find more and maybe I'll write a book about them.

A home office is a perfect place for your Personal Museum of Success. Taking pride in ones' attainments solidifies his or hers success, skills, achievements and conveys a feeling of accomplishment. What better way is there to start the workday, conduct your business in an atmosphere that supports your ambitions, and at the close of the day, an affirmation of a job well done.

"You live as long as you are remembered." ~ Russian proverb

Individuals and organizations should display their awards proudly for all to see in the office. Displaying historical items such as photographs, old documents and items from the past is a way for us to remember our history and accomplishments and to share them with others.

Awards demonstrate dominance and significance.

It shows consistent commitment to excellence. Lifetime awards never diminish. Accomplishments like these should be showcased to sparkle and shine for all to see and even offer inspiration.

Is It Time to Trash That Trophy?

Are trophies, plaques and medals no longer wanted? If you do not or can't display them in your home, then don't.

Make a space-saving digital record and take a picture of the award and put the image in a scrapbook.

Name plates that are attached to the trophy can be pried off. They are generally thin and light enough to put in the book.

Before disassembling the trophy, make sure you record the story of how and why it was received on the scrapbook page. Saving the memory it will make you smile remembering those proud moments in your life.

Donate the trophy to Special Olympics or a similar organization. They can remove the name and re-use it.

Donate them to a teacher to give them to her class for "special awards" day. Or a woodworker, vocational ED program, or a shop class at a high school, might be interested in the wood. Send them to a local theatre group or high school theatre group for use as props.

Local governments have recycling programs for metal and wood and some shops will recycle them into "new" by reworking the pieces.

Whatever you choose to do, it will be far better to know that your hard-earn trophy is being appreciated by someone else instead of rotting in a garbage pile.

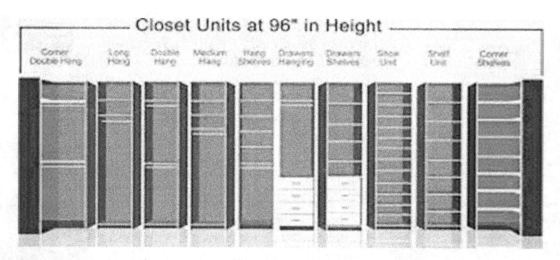

Find a closet that is not already filled to the gills? An extra closet? I have to be kidding. Right? Well, I thought the same way. My closet space was minimal and stuffed to the maximum. After bringing down the boxes from the attic, they were piled in rooms for weeks. It was a daunting task to divide and conquer, and to find everything a place and a place for it all.

The trick about taking an overstuffed closet and turning it into display space for your Family Museum is having some kind of space to transfer the closet's paraphernalia.

To meet the demands of both ample closet space and sufficient space for display purposes, invest in shelving, wall cabinets and/or module closet systems. All offer many options and designs for the closet space to be configured and adapted into a display unit. Custom-built shelves can be placed in other rooms: laundry, bathroom, other closets, the basement, attic, and the garage for storage.

Linen closets make the best space for a museum because they already have shelves and lighting.

After you cleared it out, if the shelves are wire, replace them with solid shelving boards. Replace standard sliding closet doors with decorative interior, bi-fold or French glass doors. This allows for viewing and the light from within illuminates the room and hallway.

By combining form and function with extraordinary design, reach-in and walk-in closets can be transformed into an organized display and storage of family heirlooms. If there is a room in the house that can be converted into a family museum by installing a closet system for your heirlooms instead of clothing, that would be a very creative way to create the museum. Where ever you locate your Family Museum, it will be an inspiring and charming space that will bring a visually stunning and timeless beauty to your home.

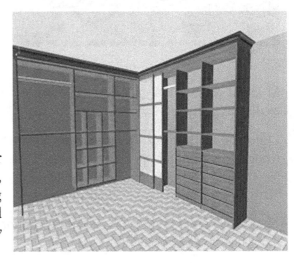

Wherever your museum resides, don't forget to hang a sign embellished with your *(Family Name) Museum.*

"You can find a lot of old memories when you clean out your closet." ~ *Anonymous*

A disadvantage in using bookcases, curio cabinets and coffee tables for family museums is space limitation. Tall or large items cannot be displayed properly. These items can be best displayed in custom-built units.

Determine the size of the items and display as a whole. (Remember selection is encouraged). Then assess the room's space, traffic pattern and furniture arrangements.

Once the space is determined, make a sketch or find pictures (many online) of what type of unit you have in mind. Allow room for pieces that are large, such as a child's wagon or dollhouse. Arrange the shelving (adjustable shelves add versatility) to accommodate tall items.

If clothing is displayed, such as a wedding gown or military uniform, allow enough room to provide space for the dress form, if you use one.

Displayed on the top shelf of our Family Museum is my husband's 1970s Leisure Suite and my 1980's (I call 'Dynasty') suit. I did not have dress forms for either, so I used some very stiff cardboard and lots of tissue paper to make the clothing free-standing. A pair of shoes compliment the pink suit.

Modular wall systems are popular. The best units are often a mixture of display and storage.

Equipped with adjustable shelving, cabinets, drawers, with glass front doors & other specialty options, these freestanding boxes can be stacked and rotated atop one another, giving ample ways to display, store and organize heirlooms.

They work where a piece of furniture cannot, allowing you to tailor the space precisely to your needs.

A Family Museum can be placed under a staircase, over a doorway and around windows. It can be built into walls and enhanced with light.

Or by removing closet doors and installing shelves, customizing the museum to your specifications.

Custom units are suited to odd size spaces and odd shaped items that need unusual configurations. Prices vary on size, materials and labor.

There are so many different places to locate a Family Museum and can be found and built with imagination and a creative spirit. Go online to see a plethora of choices and ideas that will make your head spin.

Pay close attention to the shelves back wall where you can hang photographs, plates, even small items of clothing. Styrofoam and wood blocks (found in craft stores) are good for building height. Group related items together to make a cohesive display.

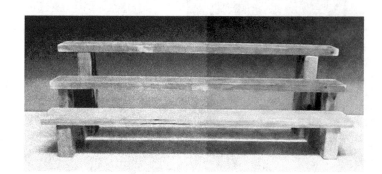

Stair-Step shelves adds display space and dimension and come in a variety of materials. (Pictured here are simple wood pieces constructed out of repurposed wood.)

Acrylic step-shelves are fun to work with because you can slide in small items under the steps to enhance what is on the steps.

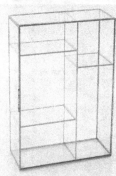

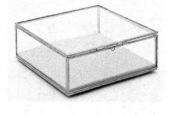

When space is tight and there are many small items that you want to exhibit in the museum, incorporate every type of display unit you can find such as clear shadow boxes. They come in many sizes and shapes, in brass, wood and plastic.

Use small easels to hold pictures and plates. All of these items come in a variety of materials, sizes and colors. In or out of the family museum, they are indispensable.

Arrange by age (baby), time (School years), career or hobby interests. Cluster a collection to tell a story.

Just as in a museum where a display conveys an historical era allowing the viewer to see a big picture of who, when and how the person, place or thing came about and contributed to the period.

In your Family Museum, the display tells your family history.

I advise leaving a good portion of space under the top shelf for storage. Install curtains or doors to conceal other items or heirlooms. A dramatic material for a curtain enhances the museum's look.

You do not have to display everything. One or two of a particular subject matter is sufficient, storing the rest. If you desire to change the display, those items are in easy reach. So now is the

time to use those boxes, bins, even the old toy box to store things away to perhaps display later, or when it is time to move, the packing is done.

Get the entire family involved with the project. You will be surprised at some of the suggestions they will make. Keep an open mind and your Family Museum will be fun for everyone.

A good aspect of living your life as a single, unattached person, has a distinction of its own. Expressions of individual taste and preference is not challenged, and one is at liberty to develop a unique style of living. If this situation is yours, what a good time for you to create a personal museum filled with cherished objects you saved, given or found, all to your liking.

 Depending on your space, curio cabinets are suitable. The shelves are glass and usually come with a grove set on the back side to place items that need to stand. If the grove is not there, use Museum Gel, easily purchased at craft stores and online. Lighting is generally installed, illuminating the treasurers.

If more room is available, a series of cabinets can be flushed together along one wall or centered between rooms to make an intriguing room divider. They are available in stores or can be custom-made to your specifications. You can also find them in second-hand and antique stores, lending the possibility of making the cabinet even more unique.

So take out those big and little keepsakes, precious heirlooms and memorabilia out of the boxes and create a tableau that represents you, your history, your passions and interests and share them with friends and family.

Think Out of the Box

(When There Is No Room in the House)

Locating your Family Museum in your home can be a challenge, especially if display space is out of the question, which poses the query: Where and what kind of space can you locate your museum outside the home? Here a few solutions to this quandary, albeit unconventional.

I have a cousin in California whose house is too small for a museum. He previously purchased a private mausoleum in a cemetery close to his home and after he arranged a small desk with a lamp and a comfortable chair, he installed a book case to display his keepsakes and for the family urns. He hung some pictures and laid a nice area rug. Now this unusual place serves as his Family Museum.

Another idea is a small storefront, and depending on the size and substance of the content, perhaps the exhibit can be open to the public and a small entrance fee required that would help pay the rent and possibly encourage other people to create their own family museum.

There are also self-storage units that come in all sizes and are available 24/7 to the renter.

Another possibility is for the family to come together in one home where there is enough room (such as a guestroom) where the families can allocate the space to create a communal museum for all the family to share. Or even this idea: the family gets together and purchases one of those tiny houses and locates it where it is convenient for the family to display their heirlooms and to visit.

Preserving Your Papers

On a Sunday I read our local Daily Press newspaper and enjoy reading the questions posed to Amy Dickinson of "Ask Amy" column. This one caught my attention, for it was a rebuttal to the advice Amy made:

Dear Amy,
You told "Clean Jean" that it would be a good idea to shred 15-year-old divorce documents between her and husband, rather than share them with her children. I disagreed. These documents become historical records and are part of a family's history. She should keep them.   *– Family Historian*

Amy wrote back: Dear Historian, You Make a great point. Thank you.

This *Family Historian* should be thanked for her astute stewardship. The information on divorce papers is a resource for family histories, as well as other papers such as birth & death certificates, last wills & testaments, military discharge papers, etc. The very thing that is most important is that all paper documents should be digitally saved, for this is the safest form, as well as in its original form or facsimile. This information is extremely vital for genealogical research and verification.

Responsible planning and management of these references is imperative and the very essence of a family is its history. When creating your *Family Museum*, try to incorporate space for special archival storage boxes that protect and preserve paper.

And for all of you like the Family Historian, thank you and keep up the good work.

Remember, the present needs to take care of the past for the future to learn.

Instead of focusing on the physical aspect of organizing, let's turn our efforts to quantifying, i.e.: purpose, vision, itemizing, detailing, cataloging, and then creating.

Objectives: the reasons you want to archive your family keepsakes. What is your motivation? Is there validation in your intention? The catalyst can be a simple incentive, such as saving that antique meat grinder of her grandmother's. Or your father's cigar box. Sit down and have a talk with yourself and then share your thoughts with your family. Saving should be fun and not burdensome. Give it, yourself and your family time.

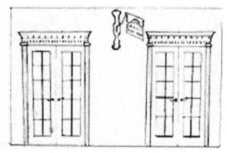

The Plan: Architects and designers start out with a vision. What's yours? Here is a chance to get back to basics by actually taking pencil, paper and a ruler in hand and draw out how you envision your archival space. Sketch an image. When my family decided to create our *Family Museum*, I sat down and drew a picture, measuring the available space along the way. Ask the family for their ideas, how they see it. Make this a family affair.

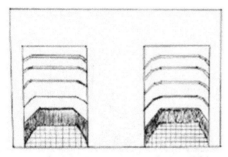

Documenting: Start by taking a photograph of each heirloom. Record which relative owned the object and tell the object's story. What is it? Who owned it? And why is it important to the family? Now create a memory Box, placing photographs in a box for each person. Organize each box starting with dates, and if no dates are found, give a good guesstimate. If needed, there are many photo-journaling sites that have a variety of online tutorials and products that offer guidance on how to document photographs. Once the boxes are filled and others are needed, make more boxes.

This is also a good time to make other Memory Boxes, for each family member filling them with odd-ball things. During our lifetimes, we accumulate many little things that mean a lot and instead of stashing them in a non-descript box, put them in the Memory Box. As a blog post suggested, give the box as a present. You will be surprised at how thrilled the owner of those things are and glad that you took the time and thought to save it for them. Hopefully, they will take it from there.

Separating: Here comes the piles! Stacks and heaps of paper, however, don't make a mountain out of a mole hill. All of these physical records can be organized, a little at a time. The importance of the papers should be considered first. What kind are they? Property Deeds, Wills, Certificates. Get file folders, title each one and put the corresponding documents in that folder. Once this is finished, digitize the paper documents.

The purpose, the rationale, the function and the intent should be foremost in your mind: that your *Family Museum* is where to . . .

"Keep all special thoughts and memories for lifetimes to come.
Share these keepsakes with others to inspire hope and build from the past,
which can bridge to the future."

~ Mattie Stepanek

Maintenance
Conservation and Preservation, Cataloging and Storage

Heirlooms, antiques, collectibles, keepsakes . . . all of them have different values, monetary as well as aesthetic. Our homes and our lives are filled with things. Some are more important and some are more valued than others. Once you have selected the artifacts to display in your Family Museum, which is a conservation project in itself, those items placed in the museum as well as in storage should be catalogued, maintained and preserved. You also need to consider the space your unit(s) will require: levels of proper temperature, lighting, accessibility and safety. Here is a guide for you to become acquainted with archival terms to assist you in this endeavor.

➤ <u>Conservation</u> protects and manages the care of valued artifacts, collections, heirlooms, etc.
➤ <u>Preservation/Restoration</u> is the repair and renovation to keep all in a good condition and safeguards precious items from loss or damage. Cleaning products must be scrutinized so that you are using the appropriate chemicals. Same with repairing, making absolute sure you hire the best restorer for your valuable heirlooms.
➤ <u>Cataloging</u> is making a complete list of all the items displayed and in storage, arranged in whatever systematic order you choose. Account ledgers are efficient books in which to log, make entries, document, classify, list, index, categorize, sort and divide inventory. Keep this information (in hard copy placed in a fireproof box and on a computer disc) for the very intent and reason for cataloging. By implementing a filing system, it will help you create your archive collection.

<u>Archive</u> is a collection of historical documents or records. We all have archives: notebooks, scrapbooks, photo albums, journals, diaries, or account books. These bits and pieces of recorded dates, places and events are extremely helpful as you assemble your displays. Filing cabinets are sufficient to store this information. Many are lovely pieces of furniture that can be incorporated into your decorating scheme.

<u>Archivist</u> – the one who keeps the records that documents the memories of the family's past, which will provide an acute understanding of the family's history. When you do this, you are establishing provenance: the history and ownership of the item(s) origination.

Maintenance
Conservation and Preservation, Cataloging and Storage

 Storage space is important for saving and keeping family treasurers. There are many types of storage units, some specific to size and shape of the item: map chests, filing cabinets and archival acid-free boxes for storing valuable photographs, artwork, or documents and precious items such as maps, prints and newspapers.

Many websites will help you to investigate, compare and learn about the different ways to protect your property. Check out the latest books on this subject at bookstores and libraries as well.

Once your archives are created and the preservation, storage and maintenance is in place, you can take pride in a job well done and take comfort in the knowledge that your family's keepsakes, collections, antiques, and other precious items are no longer obscure and forgotten. Your Family Museum(s) will be a continuous record of past events, present acquisitions, and sets in motion the preservation of future experiences.

"A place for everything and everything in its place." ~ Benjamin Franklin

"Order is the shape upon which beauty depends." ~ Pearl S. Buck

"If you don't recount your family history, it will be lost. Honor your own stories and tell them, too. The tales may not seem very important, but they are what binds families and makes each of us who we are."
~ Madeleine L'Engle, American Writer

*"Keep all special thoughts and memories
for lifetimes to come.
Share these keepsakes with others
to inspire hope and build from the past,
which can bridge to the future."*

~ Mattie J. T. Stepanek
American Poet

Just as this book was created page-by-page, so was our Family Museum, shelf by shelf. The Parent's Museum came first, item by item, and as much as could fit in it, the museum took shape.

Displaying was a challenge but most of what was significant told the stories about our family's life: experiences, hobbies, interests, careers, marriage, houses and travel. Life certainly has its ups and downs, expectations and surprises. And sadly, much of it can be forgotten.

A Family Museum is a miniature tableau that presents a bigger picture of the lifetimes displayed there, inviting you into and onto the stages of live, lived and living, offering you a moment or two to reflect on what was, what happened, and what was dreamed about and came true.

On the following pages are doors to our Family Museums. Come on in!

The first items that went into our museum were mine and my husband's baby toys taking center stage. From there, his things went to the left; mine to the right. Grouping things by age was the method I used to keep organized. It didn't always work, especially when things didn't fit or there were too many items and some had to be stored away.

As time went on and new keepsakes were found, I placed them where they belong but sometimes I ended up creating another category. After a couple of years, many of the remembrances became disarranged. Some items actually were piled on top of each other and this would simply not be tolerated. So I took most of the items out and rearranged every shelf, creating a far better display of our things than before.

One needs to be mindful and attentive with a family museum. Time moves on and possessions continue to be collected, so know that like any museum you see, small or expansive, the exhibits are always being taken care of, changed, displayed and stored. You need to do the same. After all, this is your history.

Here are a few of the keepsakes displayed in the parent's museum.

Keith's Cowboy Guns & Baby Toys

Keith at work as a building contractor

Red Racing Boat built by his father

Lizzie's Barbie Doll Kitchen Set

American Heart Gown

Catholic childhood

Potpourri of Keepsakes

The humble Baby Book has become a passing fashion. Sometimes fancy bound volumes, some inexpensive, others cheap, baby books went mass market in America beginning in the 1910s and only became more popular over the succeeding decades. But in today's fast pace world, there is a new trapping of parenthood – the baby blog. This new form of the baby book where mothers and fathers, record random thoughts about their babies, from the mundane, to significant moments, to the wondrous details of infancy. Be it book or blog, they contain useful information, keep track of things like height, weight, language, illnesses and immunizations. However, once the baby had grown up, the book and/or blog isn't needed.

Why did baby books appear around the turn of the 20th century? Well, partly because parents could finally count on their babies surviving. Sanitation improved, medicine got better, and infant mortality rates dipped sharply. As parents kept all this information on their children, it help show how families thought about the health of their children; which measurements were thought to be important, which diseases were concerns, and how these things changed over time. But as much as the books were about medicine, they were also about culture, especially when they included photographs revealing aspects of home life, such as baby clothes, furniture and activities.

How do we know these things a century later? From historians who gathered, saved, and researched the history of babies in modern America. In time, few were intended to be keepsakes passed on to generations. "Most persons regret that the little items of babyhood, so interesting to the parents at least, pass into oblivion," reads the introduction to 1889's Baby's Record: a Twofold Gift for Mothers and Children. Many baby books were only partially completed and sadly, few have been saved. The book is not intended to be a family record, but an individual one, which will form a part of the outfit of each newcomer in the household, and which can afterward to given to the child, to be preserved as a source of interest and entertainment for himself and his own children in after years. Both my husband and I have been fortunate to still have our baby books. And because we were both born in 1950, the books are quite similar. Keith's was better attended to than mine, but both are preserving our babyhoods. Do you still have your baby book?

For Keith's first Christmas, Santa gave him a toy police car (it probably had a siren that sounded when the car was pushed) and stuffed vinyl lamb. This type of stuffed animal was very popular because mom could wipe it clean after it was placed in the mouth and thrown on the floor. The car is long gone but he still has his lamb.

Years ago, his mom was in a rarified mood when she opened her cedar chest full of family heirlooms. At that time she decided to start passing on the things she saved and by doing so, enjoyed seeing the wonderful expressions of surprise and delight on her son's face when she gave him his baby shirt. The face on the shirt is of a bunny rabbit, his ears stitched in yellow and blue buttons for eyes and blue stitching for his nose and bow tie. Keith's thinks his sister did the sewing. As the shirt's material was fragile, I put it into a shadow box for preservation. I put cotton stuffing in the shirt and sleeves to give it some shape. Keith was thrilled when I presented it to him as a Christmas gift.

A selection of plastic animals, wooded alphabet blocks, his baby shoes and one knitted sock, along with a tin coffee pot and china cup is quite an eclectic collection. Most of these toys were hand-me-downs from his brother's and sister. Keith loved his two boy dolls; one with the red jacket and black pants handmade by himself with his sister's help. The little Indian boy and drum with its leather top was given to him by his uncle who lived out west. The tiny log cabin is ceramic as is the log and ax. With Keith's birthday being the same as President Lincoln's, he always had a log cabin chocolate cake for his birthday. Though they were not toys, the drawing of the train and the bunny handkerchief were from his first grade school days proudly displayed on the top shelf.

One of the oldest toys' in Keith's collection is the cowboy on his horse. It is a vintage wood and metal toy, circa 1940s called a *Steven Rock-A-Toy*. This toy was also handed down to him by his older brother. In its prime, the horse was attached to a long rod with a weighted foot attached. When you pushed the horse, the cowboy would take a rocking-good ride on his horse, his head and arms swayed along with the horse's head, moving back and forth as he rocked. The rod is long gone and the horse shows some wear-and-tear, but the cowboy is still riding into the sunset.

These are but a few of Keith's precious toys from his childhood. Now for my toys . . .

Parents Museum
Our Baby Toys

Compared to Keith's, it looks like I didn't have many toys, at least those that got saved. But what I still have are none-the-less precious.

I think all babies born in 1950 got a stuffed vinyl lamb. Mine is a bright yellow with blue and red triangles printed on the shiny vinyl. My lamb also had curly eyelashes. Putting the two lambs' side-by-side, mine looks like a girl lamb and his a boy lamb. It is truly amazing that we both had the same toy and still do.

I can't tell you why many of my baby toys were not saved like Keith's. I can't even remember having many toys, but I surely must had a few. I do recall a baby doll, but not until I was older. The first doll I truly cherished was my Barbie doll. So on my side of the museum is but a few of the baby items that were saved. Such as my ceramic baby dish.

I do not remember eating out of it. But I do recall playing with it. Just like my mom did, I put water (not hot like it is meant to have) and pretended to feed whatever baby doll I had. The dish is in excellent shape and still retains its bright colors. I did some research on the dish and found there are plenty to be had. That's nice but sad at the same time. I am happy that I still have my baby dish, but wouldn't the many others who also did would still like to have it, too? My baby shoes are still enchanting as is my baby hair brush. If I ever needed my hair for a DNA test, there is plenty of it still on it.

This photograph was taken sometime in 1952. My older brother Eddy is next to my mom Dorothy. I am being held by my dad, Bill. My mother use to say she had the perfect family, a boy for you, and a girl for me. Except, Ed was mama's boy and I was daddy's little girl. That explains a lot about my childhood. The other picture is of me on Lake Michigan beach. I wish I could remember that day. It looks like I was having a lot of fun!

Finally, my toy kitchen set that miraculously got saved. This vintage 1950s *Wolverine Tin Litho Yellow Kitchen* Stove, refrigerator and sink is rare, because when I researched this, I never saw the set in yellow. It came mostly in pink. I did see a blue refrigerator and a pale yellow stove, but never a yellow set. This must have been one of the earlier made sets by the *Wolverine Supply & Manufacturing Company (1903-1950)* founded in Pittsburg, PA by Benjamin Bain and his wife. And I think my dad bought it for me because he was from Pennsylvania and visited his brother who lived in Pittsburg. It's interesting to read that the company closed in 1950, the year I was born. I am happy the set was saved and continues to be cherished. That is what having a *Family Museum* is all about.

Two of my blog postings featured vintage clothing and what better piece for clothing to start out with than with my 1956-57 school skirt. I think I wore it on my first day back to school. I remember wearing it often, as I did not have a wardrobe of means. I think it had two long jumper straps because inside the waist band are buttons that held the straps in place. I think I remember them always falling down, too. I also had a white blouse with short puffy sleeves.

I can't remember where my mom bought the skirt, but I do remember shopping at Montgomery Ward in Chicago. We use to get their big catalogues in the mail and I remember flipping through the black & white and colored pages picking out mostly the toys I wanted. Heck with school clothes! Today with vintage clothing being popular, I wonder if there are any skirts like the one I had available for sale. There are many vintage shops online. It's fun looking at clothing you once wore. And I wonder if the clothes kids wear today will ever be considered vintage? I think not but I could be wrong. After all, fashion is in the eye of the beholder?

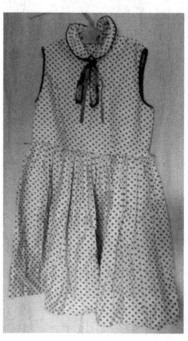

Sundays at our house were very traditional. Living in a very ethnic (Italian, Polish, Yugoslavian, Irish, Mexican) neighborhood on the south side of Chicago in the 1950s, we all had one thing in common – we all went to church on Sunday. My family was Catholic and we attended the Sacred Heart Catholic Church. Everyone dress their Sunday best. Especially on the holy days.

I loved this red, white & blue patriotic dress, at least what I remember of it. My favorite color was and still is red. And I loved poke-a-dots and red ribbons. I think this was an Easter Dress because it had a coat and hat. I no longer have the coat and hat or gloves, but somehow the dress was saved.

Here is a picture of me and my brother, Eddie, in our church clothes. What a cute brother-and-sister we were; me in my red poke-a-dot dress with its navy blue coat and little hat and white gloves! When did a little girl last wear white gloves? And him in his corduroy pants, white shirt and bow tie.

Parents Museum
Childhood Clothes

Just for the fun of it, here we are in our everyday clothes. Now, that's what I'm talking about. Gosh, we both look like we just got off the boat.

Even better than this is the one of just me. Can't imagine what I was thinking, but hey, dig those shoes! Now this outfit is what I call style . . . shabby clothes and fancy shoes. The shoes were hand-me-downs from my cousin Margy. She was a rich kid. But I had STYLE!

In my Family Museum, I do not have the space to display the few vintage clothing pieces I have. Those that are displayed are absolutely fun to see and talk about. The others are wrapped in tissue paper and stored in boxes under the top shelf. If a time came about when the subject of vintage clothing would come up, I have easy access to them. I wish I had saved more of my clothes, but alas, they are gone. However, I learned my lesson and when it came to saving my children's baby clothes and favorite outfits, I made sure I did so and now they have a fine collection of clothing memories.

It is never too late to save and if and when you pursue an antique clothing store and you see something you had as a child and would like to have it again, do yourself a favor and get it. Bring it home and proudly display it in Your Family Museum. Have fun with your memories!

I liked workbooks. At least I think I did. Both of these books taught everything that was needed to learn how to spell; vowel sounds, dividing words, open and closed syllables, vowel digraphs, derivatives, sounds, pronouncing words distinctly, etc. Several pages of spelling tests, and even a dictionary in the back. And every word was written in cursive. Not one printed letter.

Going off the tract a bit, I just read in this weekend's paper how schools are reconsidering teaching cursive. What? You mean they don't! I read that kids today are taught how to write in kindergarten (a child's brain at that age trying to learn cursive when they have yet to know how to read is unreal) and in first grades only. Then they are taught how to type! If that isn't bad enough, schools want to know what the public thinks. It asked, *Do you think children should be taught how to write cursive?*

Back to my books. It is quite wonderful to see that I was pretty good at writing cursive and my spelling ability was satisfactory. However, I can't say that about myself today. Thank goodness for spell check! As for the Spelling 8 workbook, lessons became a bit more complicated. By this time the student had to know plurals and compound words, how to analyze words, work with homonyms, word origins, suffixes and parts of speech, and of course, more spelling tests. The picture I captured from this book shows some pretty impressive cursive, but what I liked more is that I wrote with purple ink. WOW! I must have lost my blue ink pen.

I hope you liked this little trip down memory lane. Do you still have any books from your school days? I wish I had more but at least my dad saved these. Thanks, Dad.

I was not a good reader. It was much later in life that I found out why. First, my eyesight was poor and I needed glasses which I did not wear until I was in third grade. By that time my reading skills had been sadly compromised. But worse than that, I had dyslexia, a learning disability that was not recognized when I went to kindergarten in 1955. Therefore, school was always a challenge for me but I got through it. Being that I was not fond of reading, I did not like books. But my dear dad, always the saver, held onto a few of my school books that I now sentimental to me.

One of the first things you notice when you open an old book is the smell. What is it about that scent that can take you back into another time, another world? Then you feel the paper. Substantial yet now with age, brittle. So carefully you turn the pages. What is even more special is that the book has color illustrations that are vibrant and rich. These images are simplistic and innocent. Compared to today's schoolbooks, I much rather read these bygone books than the glossy, computer-perfect text and images that are produced today. So enough of my nostalgic trip down schoolbook lane and have a look at these now fondly and preserved books of my childhood.

Four books. That's all that were saved. Not much when you stop to think how many books have passed through your hands from as I went through school.

The first one was the Basic Reader (1957) titled, **We Are Neighbors** (1957). The book I had was the revised edition from the Chicago Public Library (1959). When I opened the book again, I was delighted to see that it still had the original Library Card with the earliest date due of Jul 30. Also the library card that was stamped with the due date that stayed in the book; this one dated MAR 21 1961.

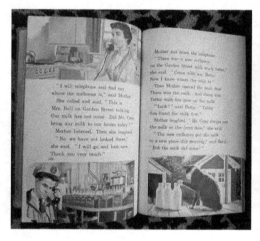

The lovely stories in the book all had to do with neighbors and neighborhoods. The sections were divided into storylines: *Garden Street Neighbors, Animal Neighbors, Good Times, Story Fun, People Who Work for Us, Round Go the Wheels, and Storybook Friends.* All of these stories with their colorful illustrations made reading fun. I can't remember if I did, but that doesn't matter because I enjoy reading them today. One of my favorites is about the Milkman. Do you remember the milkman? As the story goes, a new milkman delivered the milk to the back door when before it was delivered to the front door. Mom found this out when she made a telephone call to the delivery company. All's well that ends well. Even the cat and her kittens got their milk. When was the last time you called to find out why your milk didn't come?

The second book is interesting. Title, *All Around Me,* it is a work book prepared & published by Continental Can Company as a public service. A public service? After reviewing the 35 pages, the book is about identifying yourself, with little lessons and work pages and music.

Part one asks the reader to write "Important facts about Me, What I see and hear around Me, and what I like to do.

Part Two asks about "My Home and the people in it, what is Fun at home, What is a day at my house like, Who are helpers for the house, and The way we keep things. Part Three asks about My Town, Facts about my Town, Buildings in my Town, My School, How packaged goods come to my Town (this is most interesting because the Continental Can Company was a major packaging company), and People who work in my Town and who All my Friends are. The last page is a tear-out page with an illustration of a finger puppet with instructions on how to make it. I guess I didn't care about this because the page is still there, but with a pencil drawing of a lady that I suspect my mother drew. It certainly was not the drawing of a 9-year old.

After scrutinizing this workbook, I feel as if it was a publicity tactic to promote the can company's agenda. And I am sure the book was given to the schools for this purpose. Do company's still employ such methods? And as for the drawing of the girl jumping rope, I drew this. Other than having exceptionally long arms, I think she looks pretty happy to be jumping rope, something I did a lot when a kid.

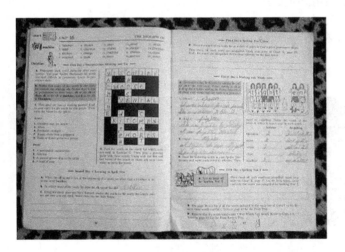

The last two books are the legendary school workbooks. Need I say more? Here are two Spelling books, one from fifth grade (1960) and eight grade (1963) both published by Laidlaw Brothers for the Catholic School Spelling Series. (My family moved out of Chicago into the country, settling in a town called Mokena. There, my brother and I attended St. Mary's School, hence the Catholic workbooks.)

Remember this day: *Oct. 26, 2014*
The Giants are one win away from their third
World Series championship in five years after
topping the Royals in Game 5 on Sunday night.

My husband Keith loves baseball (and football & basketball. Soccer, a little). His favorite teams, being born and raised in Chicago is, of course, The Chicago White Sox, and the Chicago Bears.

American Association's New York Metropolitans, who played (and lost) the first unofficial World Series in 1884 (Library of Congress)

First, a little history: Six things you may not know about the World Series
1. An unofficial championship between leagues predated the World Series.
2. The outcome of the first World Series may have paved the way for Major League Baseball.
3. The World Series has only been canceled twice.
4. Only one "world champion" team didn't come from the United States.
5. One team has won 27 World Series, while two hapless franchises haven't appeared in a single one.
6. Before the era of championship rings, triumphant players took home timepieces.

Here are the keepsakes from Keith's baseball days in our Family Museum.

Little League Ball; Baseball card of Jack Christy Mathewson (1915) found in a Cracker Jack Box; Tickets stubs from a White Sox' game. What a bargain in 1970 at $3.50 compared todays price of $125.00. And this give-away-bat from a past White Sox's game Keith and I attended. Are small baseball bats still given away? Last major league game we went to they didn't. So I guess this little bat is a rarity, therefore, belongs in our *Family Museum*. Do you have any mementos such as home-run balls, autographed pictures, etc.?

Little League's roots extend as far as baseball's history itself - even into the 18th century. Though Keith did not play in a little league, he played with the neighborhood kids in the empty field next to his house until a new house was built there.

Keith's 1958 Little League
Ted Williams Glove
from Sears Roebuck & Co

Ted Williams and Sears Roebuck partnered up with and introduced the Ted Williams brand of sporting and recreation goods in 1961. Sears distributed over one million gloves between 1960, and 1980. A Ted Williams Sears Roebuck glove is worth about $40-$75 in excellent condition. A glove in mint condition will sell for more.

Keith doesn't remember how much was paid for his glove and that really isn't the point here. What matters is that he still has it and when he slips his hand into it (the glove still fits) fond memories of playing ball out in the field next to his home are still vivid and cherished.

Keith recalls little about his days as a Pal & Pioneer with Awana. His mother was a devote Baptist and raised her family of five boys and one girl to be good Baptists. As Keith was her last child, she doted on him and made him take part in bible studies. What I find interesting is that Awana was founded the same year Keith was born and that its headquarters were in Streamwood, Illinois which is not very far from Keith's childhood hometown of Midlothian, Illinois. I can also imagine that there was much ado about this organization and those who ran it must have had a fairly large alliance that promoted Awana throughout the state of Illinois.

What Keith does remember of his days with the group was getting together with the other boys and playing baseball in the church yard. He says he didn't mind learning the bible stories and liked when the class drew pictures and sang songs.

Awana (derived from the first letters of Approved Workmen Are Not Ashamed as taken from 2 Timothy 2:15) meaning, *"Study to shew thyself approved unto God, a workman that needeth not to be ashamed, rightly dividing the word of truth. Be diligent to present yourself approved to God, a worker who doesn't need to be shamed, correctly teaching the word of truth."*

Awana is an international evangelical nonprofit organization founded in 1950, headquartered in Streamwood, Illinois. The mission of Awana is to help "churches & parents worldwide raise children and youth to know, love and serve Christ. Awana is a non-denominational program and licenses its curricula to any church willing to pay for and use the Awana materials consistent with its principles.

It really is quite remarkable that Keith's hat, membership cards from 1958 & 1961 & merit pins were saved and proudly preserved and displayed are in the family museum.

I asked my husband what was one of the many keepsakes he treasured in our Family Museum. He did not hesitate a moment when he picked up this little boy doll, not quite 8 inches tall. He has on a Chinese motif red jacket (safety-pinned on) over black pants. The reason why this little guy is so beloved is because when Keith was a little boy, he went to his older sister's home for the day and there they made together the outfit he has been wearing for over 55 years. His sister Karan was learning how to sew and she thought it would be a good idea to teach her little brother the same. Not only does Keith cherish the memory, he does the same with this little doll. Who said boys shouldn't play with dolls and learn how to sew!

In 1975 I worked at the Harris Bank in Chicago distributing the soon-to-be-famous *"Hubert the Harris Lion."* Hubert was the mascot and one of Chicago's most recognized and beloved icons. When you opened a savings account, you got your choice of either a china bank or stuffed animal.

The idea was created in 1958 by those who brought us the Pillsbury Doughboy and Tony the Tiger.

What I remember the most about this stuffed lion is the ingenious marketing. I had observed that it was the men who opened most of the savings accounts and chose the stuffed animal over the bank. And because the lion was packaged in clear wrapping, the man could not hide Hubert as he walked to work or sat on the train, thus, this free advertising created much excitement in the Chicagoland area, before the bank knew it, they were inundated with people opening savings accounts to get Hubert. Who says men are not softies when it comes to stuffed animals. To see the entertaining television ad, there is a YouTube video. Watch it. It's funny!

I was fortunate to have both, however, only the bank remains and stands proudly in our Family Museum. The large stuffed lion was given away after my daughter, who was about 5 years old at the time, deemed him to scary, especially at night. So he was given a new home. Both of these items can be found today on E-Bay.

The Wedding Album. The photographs are still lovely and tell a beautiful story, making one recall picking the date. Getting the license. Deciding on a Church ceremony or other venue. Choosing the wedding attendants. Creating the guest list. Choosing where the Reception will be? What kind of wedding cake. Flowers. Entertainment. Pictures? Rehearsal party? It's exhausting just thinking about it again. Then time goes by. Was anything saved? Where is it now? Probably in a box somewhere. But that is ok, as long as you still have it.

When I was going through all of our boxes, I did find a few things that were saved and I am sure glad it was and that those keepsakes are now in the Family Museum.

The first keepsake was the top of the wedding cake. It is a bit discolored with time, but is very special, indeed.

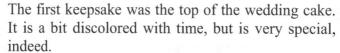

In an old stationary box I found the wedding invitations. The seven-part invites on creamy card stock with a fancy script were assembled with care and mailed out, and whoever had the best handwriting got the worthy job of addressing the envelopes. I was also amazed to find a few bridal shower invites and napkins.

Then I was absolutely ecstatic to find the receipt from my wedding dress. Yellowed with age but still legible, my mother bought my dress from *Bramson*, a high-end women's fashion store located in Park Forest, IL in the Evergreen Plaza.

I did some research and found a near-like version of my dress purchased in 1968. Asking price was $720, originally $3,500. My mom paid $113.40 for the dress, veil and tax. Of course it was the previous year's design, but I did not mind that. It was beautiful and I loved it.

My wedding gown was a *Priscilla of Boston*, designed by Priscilla Kidder, one of the most famous makers of wedding gowns in the US in the 1950s, 60s & 70s. After coming to prominence in 1956 when she designed the bridesmaid gowns for Grace Kelly's wedding to Prince Ranier of Monaco, my mother needed no more convincing by the sales lady that this was the gown for me.

Then I found the wedding dress, vail and headpiece.
The dress was an elegant floor length A-Line with hi illusion neckline with seed pearls and beadwork, and many buttons down the back and long sheer sleeves.

The very long fine net veil had a gorgeous headpiece of sea pearls and lace. I truly felt like a princess!

As for our wedding rings, we still have them but sadly do not fit our fingers anymore. But perhaps one day they will be passed onto new family members.

Note: If you do not have a Family Museum to display your wedding keepsakes, gather up what you have and put them together in a shadow box like this one. Add the wedding invitation and photographs, and hang them on a wall. It does not matter how many things you saved or how big the venue is for your heirlooms. What matters is that you still have them, protecting them, and share them now, and hopefully, pass them on to your family.

As you create your family museum, make sure you include whatever precious items you have from that time in your life. To see those things is like a gentle reminder and tells you how important was that moment in time.

Leisure Suits originated on the west coast of the US in the late-1930s as summer casual-wear for the wealthy, possibly derived from the heavy tweed Norfolk, khaki safari and Ike jackets worn by English sportsmen. Leisure Suits became popular among members of Britain's Mod subculture in the 1960s, but only achieved widespread popularity in the United States when—with the creation and popularization of synthetic materials—an unprecedented inexpensive suit featured contrasting stitching on yokes, cuffs, and elephant collars. Casual enough to be worn out of the workplace setting yet formal enough for business. They are frequently associated with that era's Disco culture. The Leisure suit height of popularity was around the mid to late 1970s, but fell from fashion in the very early 1980s.

When I presented this pastel Peach Leisure Suit to my husband, I think he rolled his eyes. But being the loving husband that he was then and still is today, he donned the suit to many family functions, taking in all the ribbing his brothers could dish out. When we unearthed the suit from one of those many stored boxes, we had a good laugh reliving that time, when current culture and fashion protested formality. Keith tried the suit on but alas,

it did not fit. However, it holds fond memories and it never fails to make a visitor to our museum guffaw when a guy sees it and recalls his own experience with his Leisure Suit.

Hot Pants were technically defined as a brief and usually tight-fitting shorts for women and girls, first popularized in the early 1970s. But Hot Pants were more than a trend. They were a sign of changing times.

First introduced to the fashion scene by Mary Quant, born February 1934. A fashion designer and British fashion icon, she became an instrumental figure in the 1960s London-based Mod and youth fashion movements. She was one of the designers who took credit for the miniskirt and Hot Pants, symbols of the social movements brought on by the 70s. Women felt that although the inseam was short, it was still an inseam and Hot Pants gave them more coverage than a miniskirt. By promoting these and other fun fashions she encouraged young people to dress to please themselves and to treat fashion as a game.

Hot Pants came in many styles, from conservative short to short-short. The rage of the fashion runways and top models, such as Twiggy, Hot Pants took the world by storm. At first they were hard to accept as clothing to be worn in the work place until Southwest Airlines adopted the style for their stewardesses in 1970. The Hot Pants fad, rage and craze dominated fashionable society. Hot Pants and miniskirts were also a gage on how good or bad the economy was doing. The old maxim was when women's hemlines rose, so did the economy. When they went down, it was a sign of difficult times were coming. Be that true or not today, fashion is still an indicator of cultural musings.

When I modeled, I did my fair share of print work posing in hot pants. From inside the studio to outdoors, it was *the* fashion. Great when the weather was pleasant, especially in Chicago, but not very warm in the frigid winters. But the boots helped and where an integral part of "the look."

Any job in the art world was a perfect environment to wear outrageous fashions. I feel a spirit is lacking in the style world today and that's why vintage fashion is popular. Not only for young people but all ages, both men and women, who desire to have clothing that is trendy and better still, made in the USA. So next time you peruse a vintage clothing shop, see if you can find a pair of hot pants. And of course, a pair of white vinyl boots to go with them!

The last time I wore my pink suede hot pants was in 1982.

Cat Eyes! That was what these eye glasses were called back in 1960, the year I wore my first pair of glasses and of many more to come. The black frame had mother-of-pearl inlays above each lens. Pretty snazzy for a 10-year-old. I look back now and regret that I never had a picture taken of me wearing these glasses. At that time I wouldn't be caught dead wearing them when my picture was taken. And not only then. When I looked through my picture album covering years from birth to thirty years of age, not one of them showed me with glasses on. Vain? I guess so. But today, eye glasses are very fashionable. So here is a little history of my eyeglass journey. Do you have any of these style glasses?

Here are most of the eyeglasses I have worn over the years. I'm sure there were more than what is pictured here, so I am glad I saved what I did. I was tempted to donate them but decided these glasses tell part of my story. It also tells a fashion story, how styles changed from big & round to slim & trim. As my age progressed, so did my vision impairments. From the beginning, I was diagnosed with Astigmatism and eventually required bifocals, making finding frames that would accommodate thick lenses a challenge. So my choices were limited, however, I did run the gamut, wearing a wide array of styles and color.

My eyeglass purchases were often. There was one time I had to get a new pair of glasses because I couldn't find my glasses. While I waited for the new pair, I had to wear my sunglasses in the house. As soon as I got the new pair of glasses, lo and behold, I found the ones that went missing. And you wouldn't believe where I found them. They were resting on top of a lamp shade that had a top vent that was set just below the top of the shade, therefore, I couldn't see the glasses.

One of my favorite pairs were the ones with the multi-color frame. They went with everything I wore! And when my husband and I went to Paris, there were so many eyeglass boutiques with stunning frames, I just had to find a pair. And lucky me, there was a buy-one-get-one-half-price, so I picked out the purple and red frames.

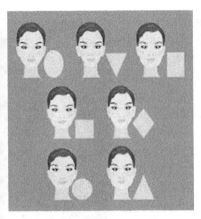

Currently, my frames are a dark purple. Pretty much in the same style befitting my oval-shaped face. According to the Vision Council, you should consider three main points when choosing an eyeglass frame for your face shape:

* Eyewear should repeat your personal best feature (such as a blue frame to match blue eyes).

* The frame shape should contrast with your face shape.

* The frame size should be in scale with your face size.

Also, while most faces are a combination of shapes and angles, there are seven basic face shapes: round, oval, oblong, base-down triangle, base-up triangle, diamond and square. A good optician can help you use these guidelines to choose your new eyeglasses.

When I researched vintage eyeglass frames, I couldn't believe how many websites there were selling all kinds of old and new frames. Just go online and type in vintage eyeglasses, and a plethora of sites come up for you to choose from. Glasses are so in style today that people wear them even if they don't have to. Must be nice, especially when it comes to all those outrageous sunglasses. So as you don your glasses, know that you are making a fashion statement. And do you notice how those looking at you through your glasses consider you intelligent. Someone told me that I looked smart in my glasses, so perhaps that changed my view about wearing my glasses, not only figuratively but actually, making me see the world bright and clear.

So *here's to* all those four-eyes (a derogatory slang for people who wear glasses) out there. Wear them proudly!

 **REVLON**

My first foray into the cosmetic world was in 1974 working for Revlon at the Carson Pirie Scott Department Store. The only experience I had with makeup was garnered from working as a free-lance model. I had no sales skills but I impressed those who hired me. With two other sales ladies, we worked the counter. Selling came easy to me and the cosmetic training we received was immeasurable. The only job I wasn't fond of was taking inventory. This stock-taking task was an undertaking. I imagine it is quicker with computerization today, but back then there were no computers. You had to count hundreds of tubes of lipstick, bottles of nail polish, and everything else that Revlon sold and it was vast. And cosmetics consultants had to sell other lines as well as their own, which meant you had to have a considerable amount of knowledge of the other products. And it was difficult not to want to sell your own line because of commission and if you were caught convincing the customer to purchase your line instead of the one they came for, you could get fired. Fragrances were a challenge to sell. You had to know the top note from the bottom note and the different strengths. How many times did you walk through a cosmetic department and some salesperson sprayed the fragrance she was selling right in your path? Many a nose was delighted and insulted. I read that this practice is now prohibited, so someone thought of a way to find out what fragrance is best for you by giving you a little test. Imagine that!

During this time, I met the Revlon Rep, Naomi. She had a glamorous job, or at least I imagined she did, traveling from store to store making sure the Revlon lines were well represented and presented. She was from New York City and of course extremely fashionable. I thought what a great job that would be, but being married and with one child, traveling was not for me. Alas, I stayed behind the counter, however, one fortunate day while I was flying to New York, I met Naomi on the plane. She was really sweet and invited me to the Revlon Headquarters on Fifth Ave in the city. What opulence! I was gob smacked. Naomi gave me a tour of the offices, even Charles Revson, Chairman of the Board, office. When we ended our tour, she autographed this book she co-wrote, writing, "Here's to being #1."

Then in 1980, my family moved to St. Petersburg, Florida. I worked as a cosmetic consultant for Clinique, a subsidiary of the Estée Lauder Companies at Maas Brother's Department Store. After completing an intense Clinique training seminar, I received my trademark white lab coat and "C" pin which I proudly pinned on my coat. I was now an official consultant for Clinique! After a year or so, I decided I had enough of cosmetic sales and turned in my lab coat but kept the pin.

Here are a few of my vintage beauty products and other souvenirs from past days of beauty: Iconic Halston Pink/Maroon Eye Shadow, Polly Bergen's Lucite Box with "Turtle" Insignia (this was one of the earlier gift-with-purchase offerings). The drawers had lipsticks & eye shadows. And this little 1965 Edition of a "Dell Purse Book" of 75 hair styles, none of which was right for me!

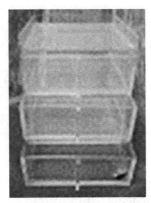

There was probably hundreds of other cosmetic bottles & containers, some very artistic & expensive, that I should of, could of saved, but sadly didn't.

So what does all this have to do with a Family Museum? Everything! The purpose of having the museum is to have a place where you can preserve and display your family heirlooms as well as your personal memorabilia. Each and every object tells a story about your life, and these few things played important roles in my life. So do the same and keep your memories alive and pretty.

Shoes! How I love shoes. What is it about shoes that makes a woman desire them so?

According to Psychology Tomorrow Magazine, *"a great pair of shoes instantly changes our mood for the better. Putting on high heels lengthens our shape, changes the curve of our posture and that physical change can evoke an inner feeling of confidence and sexiness like putting on a smile can make us feel happy. We are suddenly, taller, thinner and shapelier. A pair of stilettos pushes that all out even further.* Also, according to Dr. Valerie Steele, curator and director of the Museum at the Fashion Institute of Technology, New York. She said, *"They're an intimate extension of the body and seem to say so much about our attitudes, aesthetics, sexuality and social status."* That's good enough for me.

My first foray into designer shoes was when I purchased my first pair of Charles Jourdan shoes back in 1975. Black suede with gold & silver leather trim, and the highest heels I ever wore, a full 4" (not quite) stiletto heels. These shoes

made me tall and feel tall. At my full height I was 5'7''. Now I was 5'11''.A model's height, for sure. Were they hard to walk in? You bet!

Here's a bit of history about Charles Jourdan (1883 – 1976). He was a French fashion designer known best for his designs of women's shoes starting in 1919. In the 1930s, Jourdan was the first shoe designer to place advertisements in the high-end fashion magazines, which helped to identify his name as an haute couture house. In 1975ready-to-weat clothing and handbags were added to the Jourdan line, although the company has remained best known for its shoes. I was fortunate too own two pairs; the black ones and these pink ones.

These shoes are a luscious pale-pink shade, the mere style and cut tell you that they were special shoes, indeed! I felt like a princess wearing them.

A dear friend of mine, Donna, introduced me to shoes made by Maud Frizon. Donna insisted that I will never again feel such a comfortable shoe. But the price! I knew I couldn't afford them, but I charged them and paid them off as quickly as I could.

Here's a bit of history about Maud Frizon de Marco. Born in 1941 in Paris, France, she specialized in designing women's shoes. She began her career in the 1960s as a model for Parisian Haute Couture Houses of Nina Ricci, Jean Patou, and André Courréges. At the time models had to provide their own shoes to match the clothes designers assigned them for their runway shows and photo-shots. Frizon disliked the available shoes from other designers, and in 1969 elected to create her own and opened her first boutique in the St. Germain des Pres district of Paris.

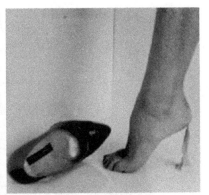

Many years ago, I was a fashion model in Chicago. I did runway, print work and conventions. This picture is from my model's book of a photographer's artistic concept for an ad for a shoe. I can't quite remember the whole story except the gum was hard to get off my foot. And I dared not put my Maude Frizon shoe back on with gum on my heel.

And let's not forget the Boots! Especially the white boots. I loved my white vinyl boots. Especially when I wore them with hot pants or short skirts. Here is a modeling photo of me wearing my boots.

In our Family Museum, I have displayed my Charles Jourdan Black Suede shoes with a vintage suit jacket. I remember wearing these shoes when I worked in a Fines Arts Gallery. I was on my feet the entire time, but for some reason, they did not hurt. I guess that is the best testament one can give a pair of stiletto heels. The thing I loved the most about these shoes was when I stood next to my 6'2" husband, I was just about eye-to-eye with him. What a powerful feeling.

Now, some 40 years later, like Cinderella's step-sisters, I can no longer slip my foot into these shoes. But because they are special to me and the memories are too good to forget, I keep the Maude & Charles shoes in their boxes. Perhaps someday, I will give them away. But you can be sure it will be to someone who loves shoes! Life is like shoes . . . if the fit is right, they will take you any place you want to go.

"Our heritage and ideals, our codes and standards – the things we live by and teach our children – are preserved or diminished by how freely we exchange ideas and feelings."

~ Walt Disney
American Entrepreneur

As a child moves through the many stages of childhood to young adult, schools, careers, travels, and relationships, they collect and save, stuffing their possessions in boxes that get shoved under their beds, piled in closets or along with yours, in the attic, basement or garage. Some of it may be thrown or given away, but then there are things that they just want to hang on to. One day they may ask you what should they do with all this stuff? You suggest that they create their personal museum.

Not only is a Family Museum a great way to teach children to appreciate their things, it is a way to install pride and confidence in themselves. When they look, touch and show off their collections – favorite toys, trophies, drawings, mementos from an organization they belonged to, gifts they received, their old eyeglasses, even their baby teeth – all show them the stages of their lives, the subjects that interested them, and the accomplishments they made. Incredibly, it shows them the learning journey they traveled, showing the paths they have taken as they mastered the subjects that interested them. Their museum is a viable resume.

Other collections may be in their rooms. The museum is a fine way for them to display their things and give them a sense of pride as they share it family members and friends. As time goes by the kids find more things they want to put into their museum. With a little rearranging more space was created for the things that would be added as time went on.

Interestingly enough, children today have far more keepsakes then we did and it is good for them to compare the difference between them. A new appreciation just may be developed along the way.

Tiffeni's Baby Toys

Sesame Street Toys

Sasha Dolls

Little House on the Prairie
Scrapbook

Career at Colonial Williamsburg

High School Jacket

Charlie's Baby Toys

Being a Cub Scout

Art work & Truck

TITANIC Collection

21st Birthday Liquor Barrels

Graduation Days

The Christening Kegs

Tiffeni posing with her keg
on April 28, 1991 at the
neighborhood's pavilion.

Charlie with his Dad, Keith,
posing with his keg
on June 12, 2008

The Children's Museum
Their Christening Kegs

On the floor of the Parents Museum (only because there wasn't enough room on the children's side) are two wooden kegs: one belonging to Tiffeni and the other, Charlie. At different times, both of these kegs were filled with Scotch liquor. When they both turned 21 years of age, Tif in 1991 and Charlie in 2008, a spigot was tapped into the kegs, releasing the 21-year old liquor, then passed around to friends and family, and all toasted to Tiffeni & Charlie coming the legal age of 21. What is the history behind these barrels? It is a Family Tradition. Never heard of such a thing? Here is the story.

This family tradition was started by my father in 1948. Being of Lithuanian heritage, Dad always told us it was a custom wherein when the first child born into a Lithuanian family is a son, the father fills a wooden keg with a liquor of his choice, seals it and buries it in the ground for 21 years. When the son turns that age, the keg is unearth and the party begins. So on September 9, 1948, my brother Edward was born and shortly following his birth, my father filled a keg with his mother's homemade Pennsylvania corn liquor. However, nobody seemed to be aware of this tradition. My mother certainly didn't until years later when dad told her about it, only because we moved out into the country from Chicago and my dad had to move the keg and rebury it out in the field behind the new house. Again, nobody but my father knew where the keg was. But he had a great time telling stories about it, getting the family excited and counting down to the day Edward would turn 21. And so he did! A very large party began. I could write a book on this event, there is so much to tell. However, this is not about my brother's keg, it is about my children's kegs, for their grandfather adjusted the family tradition when Tiffeni, his first grandchild was born. Dad decided to repeat the tradition even if he had a granddaughter and not a grandson. This time, the keg was filled with Scotch (the PA corn liquor was harsh, its bitter taste took some daring to consume, but it was), during Tiffeni's christening party. Many of the same relatives came, amused and amazed that we did it again. After the keg was filled, it was sealed and wrapped in plastic and buried in the same hole my brother's keg was. Then we moved to Florida. Tiffeni's father took custody of the keg, digging it up and moving it to Florida where he buried it somewhere in the yard. Only he knew where it was.

Eight years later, Charlie was born. Oh no! Oh yes! Another keg was filled with a Scotch selected by Charlie's dad and another Christening party was held. Two years later, we moved again to Virginia and Charlie's dad hid it in the crawl space under the house along with Tiffeni's keg. Two years later, Tiffeni turned 21, on April 28, 1991, and again, a grand celebration was had. Unfortunately, many of the relatives that were present at the previous events had passed away, but for those still with us, came they did to Virginia and with all the new friends we had a very large gathering. The keg was brought into the light-of-day and over to our neighborhood's pavilion, for we had far too many people for a house party. Tiffeni had the honors of taking the first sip, everyone watching her closely because she did not like liquor, but being the good sport she was, took a swig, declared it to be great (though she wouldn't know it if was or not) and then her parents took the next swig, declaring it fit to drink. Cups of Scotch were passed around and the party began.

The keg was emptied of the remaining contents into a wine jug, lasting a little while longer. It would be seventeen years before Charlie's 21st birthday. During this time, we built a new home and his keg was reburied on the new site. Then on June 12, 2008, Charlie turned 21 and yes, another party was given. By now, even less of the relatives were still around, but knew friends were made and all the folks had a great time as they watch Charlie searching for the keg with a pair of dowsing rods, and with a little help from his dad (who of course knew where he buried it) they found the keg. The dowsing rods came together right over the spot (funny how those things actually work) and together they dug up the keg. Untapped, a dram was poured, and Charlie took the first sip. Yum! He said. Cups were filled and the party commenced. Plenty left over and kept in a wine jug. The hole was filled and until either Tiffeni and/or Charlie decide to get married, we are sure they will keep this strange tradition alive when they have children. For now, we wait. Cheers, everyone!

The Children's Museum
Baby Clothes & Toys

What a treasure trove! Their museum has a total of, at present; 47 years for Tiffeni and 30 years for Charlie, totaling 77 years of keepsakes. When the museum was being designed, I opened the many of the boxes of the things they chose to save, and it was a blast to the past!

The hallway was strewed with toys, a large wooden horse, table and chairs, dollhouse, rolls of posters, bins of baby clothes, and of course boxes of school papers, trophies, art works, and many keepsakes.

The first items I organized were the baby clothes. And more than baby outfits. There were piles of play clothes, fancy dresses and little man outfits.

And shoes! Now these are by far the most endearing items. As I picked them up and felt the smooth leather and re-tied the laces, I floated on a wonderful flood of memories. The tiniest ones gave me much pause. Then I ran my fingers over the scuffed toes of the shoes they wore when they began crawling. Their first walking shoes made me laugh at the pictures in my head of their tumbles and falls and determination to feel the power of movement in their little legs. Even papa got a bit misty eyed when he recalled how his Tiffy would call out to him to tie the laces on her first pair of sneakers. Before I put them back in the box, I lined them up and took photos of them all.

Then came the boxes of school papers, a toy chest full of journals, and toys galore. The baby toys tell many stories, but the toys the kids really played with when they got older hold the magic of their imagination, personality traits, learning styles, and interests. As we watched our children play with these toys, little did we know then that they were the tools of their development. And most importantly, the children, now adults, can see for themselves when they pass by their museum, how important it was to save the things from their past, for it is from their past they have learned what they do in the present and take in regard what plans they may have for their future.

When a teen, Tif had a historian's heart. She acquired a passion for antiques, especially from America's pioneer years. When we lived in St. Petersburg, FL, the two of us would visit all the antique shops in town, scouring for that special find. I recall one of her first discoveries was a pair of black button-down shoes. She drove me crazy when she first saw them. She just had to have them!

After she accumulated several items, she asked her father to build her a shelf that wrapped around her bedroom for her to display her antiques. Little did I realize at that time her personal museum was created. One of her shelves was dedicated to 'Little House on the Prairie." Tiffeni wanted to be Laura Ingles, to wiggle her toes in Plum Creek and ride in a Conestoga wagon.

Tiffeni loved paper dolls, especially Betsy McCall. When visiting her grandparents during the summer, she would go up into the attic and find stacks of magazines, many of them McCall's Magazines. At first she would cut them out and play endlessly with them. As she got older and realized the value of a full uncut page, she taped them into several scrapbooks.

When older, she turned her fancies to the Victorian & Edwardian periods. She adored, "Anne of Greene Gables." She also has an unquenchable thirst for architecture. Her dream is to live in a Bungalow.

All of these interests are displayed in her side of the children's museum she shares with her brother, Charlie. Besides her *Laura* doll, there is a 'Madame Alexander' doll named *Pussycat,* and her now rare *Sasha Dolls.* Baby toys, a denim jacket covered in buttons declaring her opinion, an autographed album by Mister Rogers, whom she met while she was an historical interpreter at the Colonial Williamsburg Living Museum, and a rare Sesame Street character group. And books. Tons of books. Even a lock of her hair.

As keepsakes were added, the family museum was rearranged and in the process added space for more items, some stored. Every now and then, new-old things are added and lovingly displayed among the plethora of keepsakes that Tif will forever keep close to her heart and one day, pass down to her family.

On her side of the Children's Museum is a very diverse assortment of collections near and dear to her heart. Tiffeni's first cherished possessions where her dolls. Baby dolls were her favorite type of doll and she was a very good mother. The one pictured here is Pussycat (a Madame Alexander Doll) sitting on a Playskool giraffe. I couldn't remember when she had the doll so I asked her and Tiffeni had fun recalling vividly when Pussycat came into her life. She said, "I got her for my 8th birthday along with tickets to see "Annie." Then she went on to tell me about the other baby dolls that were gone. She said, "There was a doll named Patina and another named Patty." I actually remember Patty because she was a big doll and there was this one time when we were walking through an airport and I was carrying Patty by her arm. A woman ran up to me and scolded me for carry my child like that. I was stunned. I replied, "You mean this doll?" as I swung it around to show her. If there was a hole in the floor, she would have fallen into it. She apologized and took off. All we could do was laugh, but I can recall that moment like it was yesterday.

Next to Pussycat is her all-time favorite, Laura, made by Dolls by Pauline. Tiffeni fashioned her into a pioneer girl like Laura Ingalls from Little House on the Prairie. She was crazy for everything Little House. We even took an RV trip up to Minnesota for a family reunion, stopping along the way at every Laura site. I made this dress for her and sewed in some pigtails into her hat so she could be just like Laura. She even dipped her feet into Plum Creek, just like Laura did. Tiffeni's Little House collection is wonderful and her memories live on in the Family Museum.

Tiffeni also enjoyed reading and watching the television show, Anne of Green Gables. She has a fine collection of the books and an Anne doll that sits on the shelf with the books in her room. The other dolls pictured here are her vintage Sasha Dolls created by doll maker Sasha Morgenthaler. Boy doll Sunny, the baby in a highchair, and the girl Sasha in their original clothes. These were unusual atypical dolls, encouraging Tiffeni's colorful imagination to grow along with her.

150

Tiffeni has a wonderful collection of American Dolls. She first received Samantha for Christmas in 1986. At the time the dolls were made by Pleasant Company. Samantha was well dressed in her Victorian finery, representing an era Tiffeni enjoyed learning about. When we moved to Williamsburg, VA, Tiffeni was employed by the Colonial Williamsburg Foundation and worked as a Visitor Aide. During this time, a new doll by Pleasant Company was introduced. Her name was Felicity. There was much excitement at the living museum and Tiffeni witnessed many girls carrying Felicity around. Eventually, Tiffeni received the doll for Christmas along with many accessories. Later, she acquired the doll Molly and Kit, but by then the dolls were made by American Girl Company. There is no room in the Family Museum for these dolls, so they are stored in Tiffeni's room. Hopefully one day she will be able to display all for these dolls.

These three pictures represent her career with the CW (Colonial Williamsburg) Living Museum. Tiffeni worked there for about nine years. Her love for history and archology was nurtured on a daily basis. She wore eighteenth century costumes and collected many colonial period pieces, such as the clay bowl and mug, leather-cased bottle, a pair of reading glasses and a doll of Martha Washington. She met many celebrities including Tom Selleck, Mr. Rogers, and guided many Politian's into the Governor's Palace. She even appeared on the cover of a book titled Clothes in Colonial America with another visitor aide.

Though Tiffeni was a sort of Tomboy, enjoying playing baseball with her dad and helping him in the garden, she was and still is a fashionable gal. Her style is unconventional, mixing her wardrobe with Victorian-style clothes made by Laura Ashly, with a leather jacket and baseball cap, and when in high school, a denim jacket adorned with all sorts of patches, pins, and such, proudly declaring her diverse mind.

She also enjoyed music, her cassette player blaring out tunes by the popular artists of the 1980s. Her senior high school picture and a menu from her favorite hangout recalls those fun-filled teenage years. There is so much more memorabilia stored under the shelf, especially my old toy box filled with books and journals. An insatiable reader, a talented artist, and with her many varied interests, she went on to be a teacher, embracing the alternative educational method called Waldorf. She was very instrumental in home-schooling her brother, and later, opened her own toy store with toys from Germany. She taught art classes and eventually discovered Friedrich Froebel, the father of kindergarten, and is now developing curriculum.

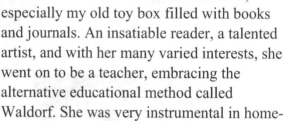

Tiffeni is a collector and saver of many things, particularly her old toys. Because display space is limited, many of her toys are under the shelves. Pictured here are three walking birds that her grandfather made. She loved playing with the musical wheels and watching Sesame Street. I found these figurines by Gorham made in Japan in 1976 (now vintage) displayed with a VHS tape and CD of Muppet music. Holly Hobby was another of her favorite dolls and the Playmobile dollhouse. She even has an extra floor and lots of furniture. All of these toys gave her years of playing pleasure and edifying value that reinforced many of her career paths. Now many of her toys are vintage and collectable and she is glad she still has them.

Charlie's shelves are loaded with all sorts of things. Baby sneakers, music boxes (he fell asleep to many a tinkling tune), endearing bronzes of his hand and foot (remember bronze baby shoes? They're gaining newfound nostalgia fueled by social media). Sesame Street dish & cup, statues & his baby blanket and stuffed animals. Bunny reigns!

His fascination with trains was overwhelming. I think every boy and girl plays with trains. Depending on the level of interest, a collection of trains can be, like it did for Charlie, take over his bedroom, down the hall, and under the tables.

He loved Thomas the Tank Trains and Brio. There were never enough Brio tracks, especially the curved ones. Eventually, there were too many trains, so he donated some of them to "Toys for Tots.

After the trains came the blimps, then submarines, followed by WWII destroyers and aircraft carriers. From there his interest turned to cruise ships, with an insatiable interest in the *Titanic*. There are models and drawings of ships, and literally tons of books on sea-going vessels and novels.

Charlie became so scholarly on the Titanic that he tried out for a part in the traveling production of *TITANIC, The Play*. He didn't get the part but because of his knowledge, the producer asked him to become the dramaturge, which is like a playwright. Charlie loved being on stage and appeared in many local productions. His favorite play was *Oliver*, because he played multiple roles.

Cub Scout memorabilia, especially Derby cars, are displayed with pride, as is his many bowling trophies. Charlie loves adding things and soon he is going to need a museum of his own.

Charlie was home schooled from the fourth grade through high school. Everyone in the family was his teacher; Papa did science and math, his sister Tiffeni taught English and history, and Mom taught art appreciation and filled in when needed. We all had a blast and Charlie kept a large scrapbook of his work. Because

of its size, it is stored behind the curtain on a shelf, along with more drawings, projects and precious memories of his school days.

In the children's museum, Charlie has a box filled with nickels. These are not just any and all kinds of nickels, they are Buffalo Nickels that many look for but few can find because they came from the World Reserve Monetary Exchange.

In 2006, Charlie saw an ad for 'bricks' of 20 special rolls of twenty-five, that will increase with value over the years. Being new at collecting coins, he purchased the Buffalo Nickels and now they sit in their special box in the museum, along with other coins. After the 911 tragedy, he purchased National Collector's Mint Silver Leaf Coin-Certificate commemorating that disaster which is in the museum.

Then recently I read this online article about the value of nickels. It said, "The value of the metal in a nickel is worth six point eight cents. According to many, it's the closest thing we have to 'honest money' . . . and people are buying them up by the truckload." So does this mean the nickel is a good investment? "Yes!"

It is recommended that people should stock up before the nickel goes out of circulation. Wonder why? The article said, "Because the prices of these metals have dropped . . . the melt value of a 1946-2014 nickel is just on the edge of four cents. Meaning, it's down well over a third of the price. Even though the metal value of the nickel is down, it is still a good investment because Fiat (sanctioned) money does well in deflation. Unlike gold, nickels have government-mandated devaluation protection. They're still going to be worth five cents no matter what. At the same time, due to their metal makeup, they are protected should inflation kick in too." So I guess Charlie's investment is a good one. And there is so much to learn about coin collecting. Here are some tips on how to stack up nickels:

Every time you visit the bank, buy some nickels. Ask them how many rolls you can buy without getting charged. Ask for new "wrapped" rolls. You could find some nickels in those rolls with minting errors. Collectors eat those things up. And they'll pay you a good return on your investment.) If you're a business owner, you'll have no problems buying nickels from commercial banks.

Go to your local casino, if gambling is legal in your state. It probably has nickel slots. Bring in a big container and ask to buy some nickels. If they haven't reverted to completely digital, you could find yourself in the money. Stop at local businesses. At the end of the day, rolls of coins have to be dropped off at the bank. It could make sense to talk managers of stores in order to have another outlet to acquire coins. Remember, all of this works great as long as the new nickels aren't released into circulation. Once that happens, you will have the same problems you have with pennies; the need to sift through them to find those with the metal content.

"Family faces are magic mirrors.
Looking at people who belong to us,
we see the past, present and future.
We make discoveries about ourselves."

~ Gail Lumet Buckley
Writer

After creating the parent's and children's museums, another museum was designed: The Grandparent's Museum: Maternal Lines and Paternal Lines. No justice was had by trying to include the few items we both saved from our parent's in our museum. These things needed a display of their own, therefore, we re-arranged the hallway which had dormer space with shelves stuffed with books. We moved the books downstairs into the home office. Then we installed and established the Grandparent's Museums. Space was tight, but after creating the other museums, I knew how to display our parent's heirlooms. Again, by forming the sides; Maternal & Paternal, everything fell into place.

We are fortunate to have the Grandparent's Museum. These heirlooms represent spectrums of their lives, their stories and memories and by having a museum, they will always be known by their Descendants. They are the reason our family exists. And by seeing everyday these family members who are all sadly gone, the museum keeps their spirits alive. So if you have a little more space in your home, create a Grandparent's Museum. It is amazing what they can still contribute to the family, for their history is your history.

NOTE on parting with the heirlooms: If a relative's age prevents them from making sound decisions as to who should get what, encourage the elder to part with the heirlooms while they are still with you. Have the elder give the item directly to the person they want it to go to or let them choose. That way they can share their memories which will make the heirloom personal and more valued.

1. Take a 30" x 46" or other size that fits your needs and space. Many of these bookcases are available at home stores and online. Some required assembly, others are sold fully constructed, however, make sure the shelves are adjustable. Material will vary from solid wood to particle board. Whatever your preference, there are many to choose from.

2. Assemble the shelves placement according to the height and shape of the heirlooms you are placing on the shelf. Consider the subject matter: who are you showcasing and what items best tell their story.

3. When I first started out, I just put all the things on the shelves to help me sort through them. As I did, the size and nature of the items gave me hints on how to display them. For instance, on the top shelf, I placed the few items I had of both my Grandparents: Lithuania on the left side, Italy on the right. The only lighting I had available was by lamp, however, there are many types of lighting you can install, such as rope lighting.

4. On the second shelf I displayed my parent's photographs at different ages, single and as a couple. The certificate in the back was given to my father by the Association of Machinist for 30 years of service. This was his profession and it afforded him to support his family.

5. The third shelf is dedicated to my dad. And he just about saved everything. This is an eclectic collection of assorted items, most having some relationship to his profession, such as his work shirt (always from Sears and in grey) that he wore when he owed a gas station, and a business card from that gas station that somehow was saved through the years. He was a builder (self-taught & built his home). He liked cigars and playing the harmonica. A pair of eyeglasses, his wallet, a collection of coins, a pocket watch, lighter, matches, and a bottle of ashes from Mount Saint Helen that erupted in Missoula, Montana on May 19, 1980 that his nephew sent him and that is granddaughter took to her 4th grade class for show-in-tell. And that's exactly what your *Family Museum* is all about, show and telling the story of a family member that honors their past.

6. The fourth shelf is dedicated to my mother and her Italian family. Mostly photographs of her, her siblings and cousins. The few items are her hand mirror, religious statues, book of memories, and a photo of her Brother Mike's auto repair business located on the south side of Chicago. He loved cars and boasting about taking care of some of Chicago's nefarious gangster's cars. There is also Mike's World War I Victory Medal for his service in the United States Military, in which he fought, was wounded, but thankfully returned home. The bronze medal features a winged Victory holding a shield and sword on the front created in 1919 and awarded to any member of the U.S. military who had served in the armed forces between 1917 & 1920 in 13 locations. My uncle served in France.

7. The bottom shelf displays a rarified grouping of my dad's things, some of which I haven't the slightest idea what they are and will never know, along with the things I do, such as the chucks of coal from his coalmining days in Pennsylvania, along with his miner's steal canister wrapped in an orange leather case my father strapped to his belt before he went down into the coal mine. It was called a *self-rescuer*. It was an air filter with a breathing apparatus that he would use in case of a cave-in. I wish I had more of his things, but what I do have I will cherish forever.

That's it. A simple bookcase turned into a *Family Museum* that displays & protects two generations from two countries who came to America and contributed their talents and produced future generations to carry on their legacy.

Liz's maternal grandparents were from Calabria in southwest Italy, a region of rugged mountains, ancient villages and dramatic coastline that occupied the "toe" of the country's boot-shaped peninsula. Thomas immigrated to Chicago in 1900 and work on the railroad. Elisabetha, affectionately called Nana, followed two years later. They settled on the south side of Chicago, raised a large family. Nana became a US Citizen in 1950. Their youngest daughter was my mother. They operated a neighborhood Italian grocery store. Not many heirlooms were saved, but what was is wonderful.

Elisabetha & Thomas Albano 1942

Photograph of Nana proudly standing behind her store counter.

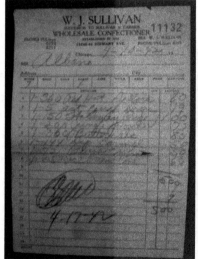

Receipt for store candy   Nana's meat grinder

"People will not look forward to posterity who never look backward to their ancestors."
~ *Edmund Burke*

Paternal Lines
The Yuknavichs

Liz's paternal grandfather, Anthony Yuknavich, was born in Uzubalici, Lithuania (at the time of his birth, this area was part of Russia). His father did not want Anthony to go into the Russian Army so he bought him a ticket to America in 1907. Anthony settled in Portage, PA where he worked on a farm and in the coal mines.

In 1917 he met and married Anna, who immigrated from Vilkoviskis, Lithuania. She had no formal schooling but was artistically talented. She made carpets on a loom that was in the attic of their home, situated in a valley in the Allegheny Mountains. Anna got her citizenship papers in 1945. They raised a large family, their eldest son was my father, William.

A few precious heirlooms remain that my father brought home after he and his mother Anna went to Lithuania to see her family. Among them were photographs, a hand-painted Easter egg, symbolizing creation, fertility, and life. Having one in the home afforded its owner protection from life's disasters and brought luck and fortune.

He also brought back stringed Baltic Amber beads. They are translucent fossil resin exuded from ancient conifers 60 million years ago and found on the shores of the Baltic Sea. Often plants and insects were trapped and preserved in amber pieces. Amber was not only used for jewelry, but it was also carved and displayed as a decorative object. Some people believe the beads had healing properties.

Juostos sashes are traditional folk costumes from Lithuania. Anna's is about 9 feet long, 4 ½ "wide, black, green and red wool with long fringe.

This is a precious photograph of my Gramma Anna & Grandpa Anthony sitting at a picnic table, content and happy to be with family & friends.

My Dad
William Yuknavich/Sommers

My dad, William Yuknavich (he changed his name before his marriage to Sommers), sadly passed away in 2004, but there is hardly a day that goes by that I do not recall him in some way. It's the little things like his off-the-wall witticisms. He was good at using them, such as the popular Midwest adage, "Oh, go jump in the Lake!" (Lake Michigan, that is), Or this one, Oh, go scratch! And when I would get hurt, a scraped knee or a fall off my bike, he used reverse psychology and told me, "Do it again. I didn't see you do it the first time!" That would get me so mad, but he would smile and made sure that I was alright. His smile was so genuine and his heart knew no bounds.

The one constant characteristic about Dad is that he saved everything. Before hoarding became part of our lexicon, I remember living with piles of things, from boxes and newspapers reaching the ceiling, walking carefully around more piles of things. My mother would have a hissy-fit, but he turned a deaf ear. So, through the years, his stuff crowded every space imaginable. When push came to shove, and by virtue of relocations, much of his stuff disappeared. What remained we saved as much as we could, looking through tons of boxes and bags, coffee cans, where ever Dad could find a space to stash things.

As we investigated, we found the treasures. Boxes filled with oddities, like his coal miner's breathing protection equipment for gas detection and lantern. He even saved a chuck of coal. Dad was a coal miner in Pennsylvania. He despised the work and as soon as he could, he joined the Navy. A veteran of WWII, he was on the USS Enterprise when it was hit by Japanese kamikaze, surviving by his wits alone. Later in his retirement years, he wrote about his life. I would see him sit at his desk and handwrite his thoughts. He had extremely fine penmanship. But he would not talk or share his writings.

Among these treasures were those writings. If they were not found, I would have never known so much about that part of his life he wouldn't talk about.

Just before he passed away, I presented him with a hefty notebook filled with his papers, photographs and keepsakes. As he turned the pages I watched for his reactions. Not as many as I would have liked, and he was still hesitate to talk about it, so I gently encouraged him to tell a little of the story, of which he did, but after a while, he became tired, closed the book, patted the cover and handed back to me. He said thank you, got up and left the room.

I'm sure it was difficult as well as pleasant for him to see his life pass him with each turn of a page. But at least he knew that I cared enough to save his history and keep it safe for his family and future generations, because everyone should know my father' story.

I have yet to finish it, as I am still finding paraphernalia I insert in the album. I offered his story on my blog and have more to write, for my father's story is always alive and well in my heart.

My Mother
Dorothy (Albano) Sommers

When my mother, Dorothy, would walk into a room, everyone was always delighted to see her. It was apparent to me even early in my life that mom was the life of the party. She exuded charisma and charmed everyone she met. Dorothy was playful and animated. She loved going to the movies and as I got older, thought that she had missed her calling. She should have gone to Hollywood. She would have been a star.

Raised in Chicago by a loving Italian mother; her father passed away when she was young, and a large family of brothers and sisters. Her mother, Elisabeth, owned and operated a neighborhood grocery store. There, Dorothy learned how to sell, keep books and engage people in conversation. She went onto college where her sisters went, but she was not fond about school. She was crazy for the movies and loved to dance. As I learned her story, I concluded that my mother missed her calling. She should have gone to Hollywood. During WWII, Dorothy joined the USO, The United Service Organization founded in 1941, in Chicago and volunteered as a dancing partner for the servicemen that were stationed or training at Great Lakes Naval Station. She with many other women provided morale to the service members by dancing and socializing with them.

There were two fancy ballrooms in Chicago; the Trianon which resembled Louis XIV's palace in Versailles and The Aragon, designed to resemble the courtyard of a Moorish castle with twinkling lights in the ceiling. I actually remember the Aragon, having danced with my father when he and mom took my brother and me to show us where they met. She told many stories about this time, in particular meeting my father in 1945.

Dad joined the Navy in 1942, serving until 1946. During that time they wrote letters; sadly many of them perished but dad saved what he could. I read the letters and they reflected their desires and fears. After he was discharged, they married in 1948.

Bill and Dorothy were married for 56 years. Dad passed away in 2004, Dorothy, 6 years later. Two children & two grandchildren, my family inherited what they had and those keepsakes are preserved in our Family Museum, keeping

their memories alive and ready to be passed down to the next generation.

Maternal Lines
The Jorgensons

Keith's maternal grandparents, Anthon & Hannah Jorgenson, were both from Finmarken, Norway near the Arctic Circle. When Keith participated in the Geno Project, he discovered that this ancestors are related to the Sami people of Arctic Europe. Livelihood for a semi-Nomadic is reindeer herding.

In 1864, three related families immigrated to America, settling in Artichoke, MN where they built homes and farms and were active with the Baptist Church. In this photograph, Keith's mother, Gladys, is held by her father. His Uncle Hans wrote this book, *"History of three Lines of Ancestors and Their Descendants," The Hanson – Jorgenson – Robertson Genealogy"* in 1971, tracing the ancestral lines of all three families.

His Aunt Alice was a Medical Missionary in the Belgium Congo under the American Baptist Foreign Mission Society from 1929 to 1960, collecting many African items, some of which Keith inherited and are now in our Family Museum.

After Keith's grandparent's passed away, the house and farm were vacated and none of the next generation wanted it. Before it was demolished, we visited the old homestead and rescued what we could. Trim work from the front porch, a brass doorknob, and a chair and newel post, which we incorporated into our own home.

Bestafar & Bestamar

"When an elder dies, it is as if an entire library has burned to the ground."   *African saying*

Paternal Lines
The Goesels

Keith's paternal great-grandparents, Christian & Dorothea Goesel, immigrated to America from Weiberstadt, a very small village in the region of Thuringia, Germany and established a homestead called *Goeselville* on the northern Indian trail in Illinois 1868, also known as "wilderness country" dating back to the 1830s. There were three factors attributed to the movement of settlers: a treaty with the Black Hawk tribe, access to a U.S. government land office in Chicago and an abundance of cheap land. Welcome to Goeselville.

Christian Goesel and his wife, Dorothea, had a grocery and farm implement store **and post office that served the pioneering families until 1909.**

At its peak Goeselville was home to 30 people and was visited by many more because of its strategic location on the main wagon road and was even a stop on the pony express route.

But when the Rock Island Railroad bypassed Goeselville and routed its tracks through neighboring Tinley Park, Illinois, the town's development opportunities were effectively foreclosed.

The town is gone now. All that remains today is the barn, still withstanding the test of time. No heirlooms were saved but a few photographs and a brochure that tells a good American story.

Pictured here is Christian and Dorothea Goesel with seven of their ten children: Louis, Minnie, Emma, Katie, Ed, Berthold, Charles, Christian, Mary and Amelia.

Charles was Keith's father's father, Marvin Goesel.

*"Do not forget the things your eyes have seen
or let them slip from your heart
as long as you live.
Teach them to your children
and your children's children."*

~ Deuteronomy 4:9
New International Version

Grandparents Museum
Great Aunt Gitta's Doll

In our Maternal Grandparent's Museum, sitting on a handmade wooden suitcase that actually is designed as a portable table (you open the case and flip out the four legs and turn it over and it becomes a table) designed and made by Keith's Bestafar (Norwegian for Grandfather).

A porcelain doll dressed in a satin gown with pink ribbons and a lace cap on her head, she sits, her head resting on a pillow with a cotton blanket tucked in around her, in a hand-made doll cradle constructed of pine and fir wood, made for Keith's Great Aunt Gitta when she was 4 years old in 1870 in Tromso, Norway. The fragile wood is smooth and it has a gentle teeter totter when you rock the cradle.

Aunt Gitta traveled with her family to the United States, settling in Artichoke, Minnesota. There it stayed until it was passed down to my husband's mother in Illinois. When she passed away in 2007, it was passed down to my husband. It now sits pretty in our Family Museum.

It is quite awesome when you figure out how many miles this cradle has traveled and how old it is. Doing the math, it traveled 5,194 miles and is 145 years old. WOW! Now that's what I called preservation!

During the summer of 2016, an envelope was sent to my husband from a cousin on his Norwegian side of the Family. There were many photographs, family tree information and a long-forgotten typed note letter to Keith from his Aunt Alice, dated 1955. Keith was five years old. The letter is framed and our museum and forever cherished.

Here it is . . .

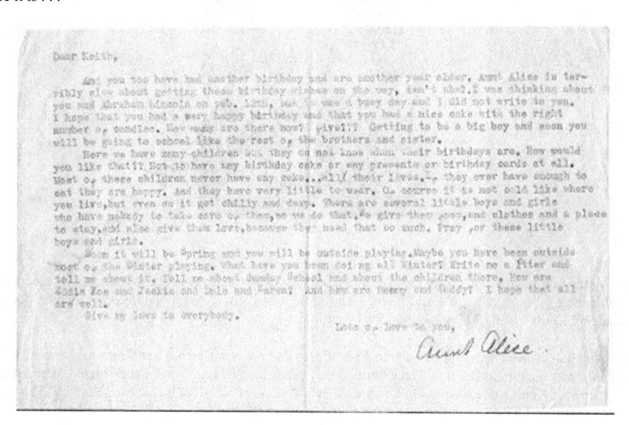

Alice's parting sentence asked Keith to write back telling her about his "Sunday school and about the children there." This reflected Aunt Alice's profession – A Medical Missionary in the Belgium Congo under the American Baptist Foreign Mission Society from 1929 to 1960. She sadly passed away in 1961. Here is a short biography taken from her obituary:

Congo News Letter
MARCH 1958

Alice Jorgenson was born May 21, 1895, and raised at Artichoke, Minnesota. Besides her public school education, she took training at Bethel Academy in St. Paul. After completing a course in nurse's training at the University of Minnesota, she took Theological training at Northern Baptist Seminary in Chicago. In 1928, she sailed for Europe and took up further training in medicine and languages in London, England, and Brussels, Belgium, before sailing for Africa. She served as a medical missionary in the Belgian Congo under the American Baptist Foreign Missionary Society, In July of 1960, she was evacuated during the Belgian uprising and was flown and was flown back to the United States. Being past retirement age, she did not return to Africa where her heart really was.

During her years in the Congo, Alice collected and was given many African items, some of which Keith inherited and are now in our Family Museum. I asked Keith what he recalled most be about his Aunt Alice, and he said, *"During one of her visits back home, she had an Ivory statue of a water buffalo and told me a story about it while I held it, telling me to be very careful with it."*

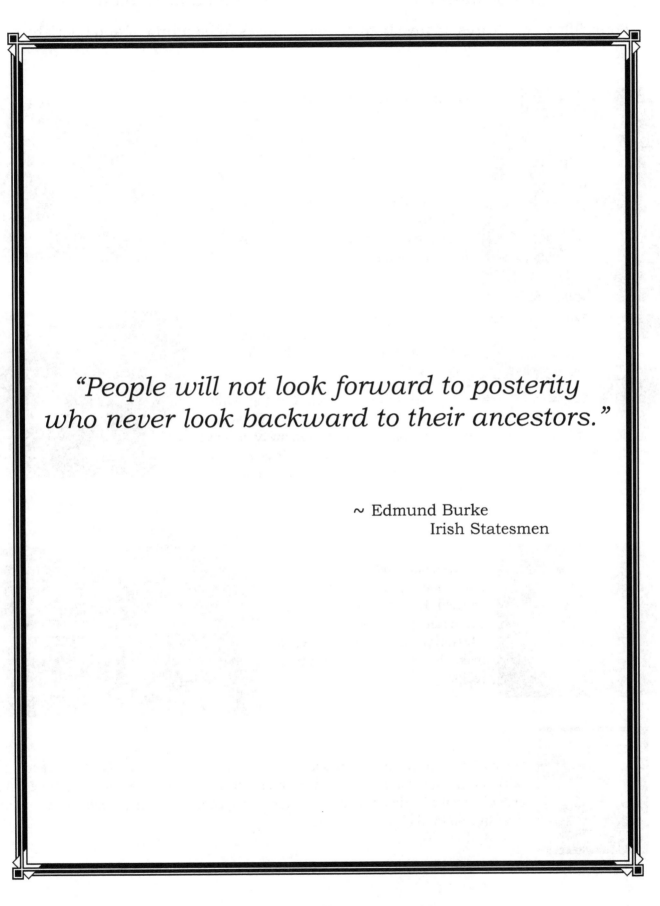

"People will not look forward to posterity who never look backward to their ancestors."

~ Edmund Burke
Irish Statesmen

Four different cultures, many customs and legacies to be proud of and cherished

Grandpa was German; Grandma was Norwegian. The melding of customs created an affectionate bond, loving memories and precious keepsakes.

Grandpa Marvin was a home builder. With his inherited carpentry skills, he built two of his homes and helped his four sons build theirs.

He was also a toy maker. During the Depression, he made wooden trucks and sold them at the local hardware store.

All of his children & grandchildren received a truck for Christmas.

Charlie & Tiffeni each have a truck. Before Marvin passed away, he gave his truck drawings to his son Keith, and now he makes the trucks and other toys. This innate carpentry skill lives on. Keith built his homes, his woodworking talent evident within.

Gramma Gladys was a professional cook for the Land-O-Lakes Family in MN before she married. Her domestic skills were extraordinary, particularly at Christmas time when she would make her traditional Norwegian recipes.

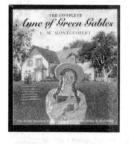

Gladys loved American history and adored all the *Little House on the Prairie* and *Anne of Green Gables* stories, which she shared with Tiffeni. There is so much more to tell and with all the heirlooms and keepsakes displayed in the Grandparents Museum, their lives live on for their Grandchildren

Four different cultures, many customs and legacies to be proud of and cherished

Grandpa was Lithuanian; Grandma was Italian. Their worlds were quite different, but blended into a lifetime of accomplishments and memories.

Grandpa Bill was a self-taught man, yearning for knowledge and achievement. Trained as a machinist in the Navy, he worked for major trucking companies making a very good living. His desire to build a home was a dream come true, resulting in a magnificent house he built from the ground up.

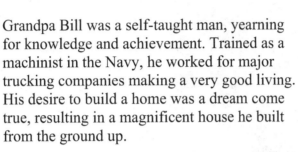

Unfortunately, not many Lithuanian traditions have been passed down. But he kept many letters and photographs of his family. He was a quiet man and though he kept private his memories of WWII, when Charlie developed an interest in naval history, he shared this pursuit of knowledge with his grandson. His desire for independent pursuits for education influenced his granddaughter.

Dorothy, affectionately called, Gran-Gran, was always the life of the party. She loved to dance (she meet Bill at the USO) and entertain. Holidays were celebrated with lots of Italian food and relatives.

Talented in many ways, she had clever and canny ways of decorating. She liked to make doll clothes. (Barbie dresses for Liz and when Tiffeni was in her *Little House phase,* she made Laura dresses.) She had a spirited way of telling fairytales and stories with flair, somehow passing this ability onto Charlie, who loves to tell stories. Again, there is much more to share, yet words are not enough. All the keepsakes in the Grandparents Museum will continue to offer their grandchildren memories for a lifetime.

"What will happen to all of the family heirlooms in the Family Museums," our kids, Tiffeni & Charlie asked. "It's all yours!" we said. "And what are we suppose to do with all this . . . they didn't quite say stuff, but I could tell that word was on their tongues . . . this memorabilia?" Not wanting to make them feel overwhelmed and so concerned about it all to the point that they were going to worry about it, I said, "When that time comes, I am sure you two will know what to do."

And so it goes, this conversation said here as it is said in many homes by many family members, wondering what to do with this - yes I'll say it, "Stuff!"

What is so important about this stuff is that it represents a lifetime, different eras and periods of history, an account, a description, an interpretation of past and present lifetimes.

The stuff in our Family Museum validates the progress of our ancestors development, from European imigrants, to United States citizens, working and thriving to make a better life for themselves and their children.

Our Family Museum was created as a way and means of how to hold onto family heirlooms. The concept was adapted from observering the exhibits in museums, large and small with collections massive and intimate.

And everybody wants to keep some things. Especially those things that shows the stages of a persons development, from childhood to adulthood, the progress that was made and the talents engaged, and all the education garnered by this growth, with the desire and hope to share it with the world at large to make society better as a whole.

Our family's next generation have much to look forward to. With the solid foundation they have been raised on, with being nurtured to appreciate the generations that came before them by virtue of the Family Museum, by respecting the very things that their ancestors worked hard for and the care they took to pass them on, Charlie and Tiffeni can point to their future with confidence. They know that notwithstanding the fact they will inherit the task of maintaining their family's past, it is up to them to take the responsibility to make sure their Lineage continues to have a presence, furthering the staying power for the next of kin.

In Conclusion

What appropriate methods are there for enabling individuals to discard and organize family heirlooms without deleting huge swaths of human history?

What is the responsibility of the individual in determining when your family heritage is worth saving?

Whose job is it to keep and preserve these memories?

If not the owner, then whoever they are, they will be accountable for the loss of those objects and the memories that are attached to them will vanish and become lost to the next generation.

There are many implications that can cause negative results through the desire to de-clutter. When something is discarded, that void will never be filled again unless it is filled with a duplicate, which in itself, is acceptable. Then you attached the memory to that object.

Isn't the whole point of collecting and preserving evidence of our past is so that we should not forget? We all have a legacy to pass along. Let it not be one mired in basements full of dusty, forgotten boxes.

By creating your Family Museum, those treasures represent a significant material genealogy you leave for your children. Not only is it a way to honor those who came before us who initiated the family heritage, the mere idea of being able to hold that memory in your hand, recall and talk about the memory, sharing it with loved ones and friends, and perhaps, you will inspire not only the family to carry on their heritage, but for others to start saving theirs, too.

I wish you the best and may God speed. Time is of the essence and there is no better time than now to start your Family Museum.

Respectively,

Elizabeth Goesel
Family Museum Curator

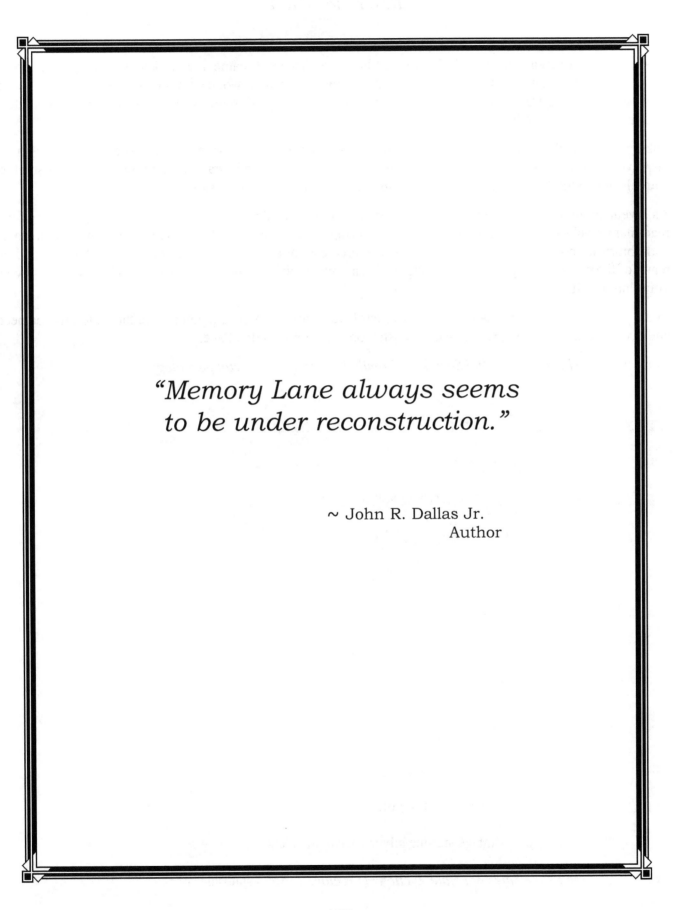

*"Memory Lane always seems
to be under reconstruction."*

~ John R. Dallas Jr.
Author

Reference Guide

When I started to create our Family Museum, I had one concept. It came after I visited the Reynolda House Museum of American Art in Winston-Salem, NC. I thought what a wonderful idea this would be for me to adopt and re-configure for my needs when I created our Family Museum. I also observed how the visitors enjoyed gazing at these family treasures.

Taking this model and the knowledge I retained from visiting museums, and how store and antique shops displayed their artworks, collections, clothing, etc., I had enough understanding on how to group, assemble, compile and exhibit my family's heirlooms, antiques and personal possessions.

As I went about designing the museum, I researched companies that specialized in how to display things and read many books on collecting, preserving and storing. And as much as I searched the Internet, book stores and libraries, I could not find one book on how to create a home museum, therefore, I wrote this one, adding many of the posts that appeared in my blog, including many photographs and instructions how you can create your Family Museum.

In the process, I discovered many online resources listed here that will help you to find the materials you need and give you ideas as well. The images are listed on the Photo Credits Page.

Good luck . . . Have Fun . . . And Save Your Family History and material genealogy!

http://www.micro-mosaic.com/micromosaic_consulting_services.html

http://www.digitalpreservation.gov/

http://www.familytreemagazine.com/article/getting-the-word

https://en.wikipedia.org/wiki/Ancestry.com

https://genographic.nationalgeographic.com/about/

http://www.genealogybank.com

http://www.ancestry.com

https://www.myheritage.com

http://www.antique-marks.com

http://latimesblogs.latimes.com/jacketcopy/2010/06/the-hidden-history-of-baby-books.html

http://rembrandtcharms.com new silver & gold charms & bracelets

http://www.rubylane.com Vintage sterling silver charm bracelets

FYI: Visit online *Estate Sales & Estate Auctions Directory* http://estatesales.org

http://search.ancestry.com/search/db.aspx?dbid=1265 on HS yearbooks

http://www.thepeoplehistory.com Vintage children's clothes

Harris Bank - "Free Hubert" (Commercial, 1981) - YouTube

Professional organizer Scott Roewer coined the phrase, "Art of Rearrangement."

Coin collection and preservation. http://www.home-museum.com/hobbies/Coins/coins.html

www.facebook.com/FloralKeepsakesBoutique (shadow box examples)

http://www.sasha-dolls.com/index.htm

http://curtdanhauser.com/AG_Collecting/Main.html

http://www.ntlibrary.org

https://monicapare.wordpress.com/2014/01/15/how-to-make-a-t-shirt-quilt-for-dummies/

https://www.awana.org/

Illustration Credits for Images

The majority of photographs are property of the Goesel Family and can be found on the Family Museum blog spot. Many graphics were found searching the web and using google images. Web sites provide more information as well as web sites listed in the Reference Guide.

What Is a Family Museum?

Art Institute of Chicago – http://www.artic.edu/aic/collections/artwork/656

Museum case - http://www.auroracolony.org

Mom & Dad Things – http://www.howtocreateafamilymuseum.blogspot.com

Foreword

Genealogy Poster - http://www.eventkeeper.com

Our Baby Toys - http://www.howtocreateafamilymuseum.blogspot.com

Our Story

Boxes in the attic - http://www.howtocreateafamilymuseum.blogspot.com

Liz's Baby shoes - http://www.howtocreateafamilymuseum.blogspot.com

Boxes - https://images.google.com

Reynolda House Rooms & Museum items - http://www.reynoldahouse.org

All stairways - http://www.howtocreateafamilymuseum.blogspot.com

3 Etchings of Family Museum - http://www.howtocreateafamilymuseum.blogspot.com

Why a Family Should Have a Museum

Pocket watch - http://murrayandmathews.blogspot.com

Whose Things Belong in a Family Museum?

All pictured items - http://www.howtocreateafamilymuseum.blogspot.com

Remember the Family Pets

All pets & pet items - http://www.howtocreateafamilymuseum.blogspot.com

When Should You Start Your Family Museum?

Hour Glass - https://www.google.com/search?q=hourglass

One Generation

Do You Remember Book - http://www.terapeak.com

Dad's Coal - http://www.howtocreateafamilymuseum.blogspot.com

Nana's Pan - http://www.howtocreateafamilymuseum.blogspot.com

Lace Doily Page _, http://www.needlenthread.com

Illustration Credits for Images

A Millennial Learns How to Save

All pictures of Charlie & items - http://www.howtocreateafamilymuseum.blogspot.com

Keeping Parents Treasurers

Sign "Change Ahead –https://images.google.com

Charlie's Bowling Trophies - http://www.howtocreateafamilymuseum.blogspot.com

Tiffeni's card box - http://www.howtocreateafamilymuseum.blogspot.com

"Storing" sign - https://images.google.com

3 Black garbage bags - https://images.google.com

Genealogical Research

Genealogical Tree - https://images.google.com

Family Tree –https://images.google.com

Family Trees and DNA

Ellis Island - https://en.wikipedia.org/wiki/Ellis_Island

Family Tree - https://www.template.net/business/family-tree-templates/family-tree-template/

My Family Tree - https://images.google.com

Roots - https://images.google.com

DNA Spiral - http://preventdisease.com/images/dna.jpg

GENO Kit - https://shop.nationalgeographic.com

Map of Germany - http://www.worldatlasbook.com/germany/germany-political-map.html

Map of Norway - http://www.worldatlasbook.com

Map of Italy – http://www.worldatlasbook.com

Ancestry.com Kit – https://www.ancestry.com

Map of Lithuania – http://www.worldatlasbook.com

Rope –https://images.google.com

Generation Tree –https://images.google.com

Collecting v. Saving

Piles of books – http://theactivescrawler.blogspot.com/2012/02/note-on-collecting-vs-hoarding.html

Library Bookcase - http://www.howtocreateafamilymuseum.blogspot.com

Messy Attic - https://images.google.com

Illustration Credits for Images

<u>*Desirable Ownership*</u>

All pictured items - http://www.howtocreateafamilymuseum.blogspot.com

<u>*The Comfort of Things*</u>

The Brain – https://gigaom.com

Paper weights – https://www.pinterest.com/pin/820640363320177073/

Relationships – https://strengthscopeus.com/strengthen-your-relationships-and-get-more-done/

Happy People – https://www.shutterstock.com/image-photo/happy-group-diverse-people-friends-family-234036376

<u>*Memory Boxes*</u>

All cards & boxes - http://www.howtocreateafamilymuseum.blogspot.com

<u>*I Wish I Would Have Kept*</u>

All pictured items - http://www.howtocreateafamilymuseum.blogspot.com

<u>*Where Items Can Be Found – Diamonds in the Rough*</u>

All pictured items – https://images.google.com

<u>*At Auction*</u>

Auction Gallery -   https://images.google.com

Antique wooden statue - - http://www.howtocreateafamilymuseum.blogspot.com

Vintage diamond ring - - http://www.howtocreateafamilymuseum.blogspot.com

Rare pen & ink sketch - - http://www.howtocreateafamilymuseum.blogspot.com

Box Lots at auction – https://images.google.com

Silent Auction – https://images.google.com

Online Auction – http://istart.co.nz/nz-news-items/online-auction-competition-heating-up/

Sold sign – https://images.google.com

Old London Auction print – https://images.google.com

<u>*At Estate Sale*</u>

All pictured items – http://www.howtocreateafamilymuseum.blogspot.com

<u>*At Antique Stores and Malls*</u>

Hoosier Cabinet - http://tparty.typepad.com/

Antique Toys - https://images.google.com

Vintage jewelry - https://bygonesvintage.com/

Illustration Credits for Images

At Garage and Yard Sales

All signs – https://images.google.com

All toys - https://images.google.com

At Pawn Shops

Queen Isabella – https://en.wikipedia.org/wiki/Isabella_I_of_Castile

Three Gold Balls Sign – https://en.wikipedia.org/wiki/Pawnbroker

Pawn Broker – http://www.mlive.com

What Should Be Saved - The Times of Your Life

All pictures items – http://www.howtocreateafamilymuseum.blogspot.com

Cradle – http://decormedley.com/baby-furniture.html

T-Shirt Quilt – http://www.goosetracks.com/T-ShirtQuiltInstructions.html

Scrapbooks

Scrapbook – http://www.howtocreateafamilymuseum.blogspot.com

Photo Albums

Newspaper cartoon – http://www.gocomics.com/closetohome

All Goesel Family Albums – http://www.howtocreateafamilymuseum.blogspot.com

Charm Bracelet

Gold Charm bracelet – https://www.pinterest.com/pin/231372499582324406/

Liz's charm bracelet - http://www.howtocreateafamilymuseum.blogspot.com

Silver Charm bracelet – http://howtocreateafamilymuseum.blogspot.com/2015/07/charm-bracelets-mini-museum.html

Pandora Bracelet – https://www.pinterest.com/explore/pandora-charm-bracelets/

Christmas Charm Bracelet – https://www.etsy.com/c/vintage/jewelry/bracelets/charm-bracelets

Bubble Gum Charm Bracelet – http://vintage-charm-jewelry.com/vintage-gumball-charms/

Auntie Mame scene- http://www.threemoviebuffs.com/review/auntie-mame

School Days

Chalk Board – http://www.marx-brothers.org/marxology/images/schooldays.jpg

Rural students – https://s-media-cache-ak0.pinimg.com/236x/85/9d/bb/859dbb7ad970183454d2d252db9fee2d.jpg

All other items – http://www.howtocreateafamilymuseum.blogspot.com

Illustration Credits for Images

High School Yearbooks

All Yearbooks – http://www.howtocreateafamilymuseum.blogspot.com

Class Rings and Class Trips

Both rings – http://www.howtocreateafamilymuseum.blogspot.com

Teen couple – https://www.amazon.com/Lemax-Harvest-Crossing-Collection-Figurine/dp/B0043B8NVK

Skein of yarn – https://www.pinterest.com/kristinpaullet/memories-growing-up/

Ferris wheel – https://www.google.com/#q=amusement+parks+in+illinois+and+indiana&*&spf=1

Swimming pool – https://www.google.com/#q=amusement+parks+in+illinois+and+indiana&*&spf=1

Going to the Prom

Dancing at the prom – https://www.pinterest.com/stephenaxelrad/senior-prom-1950s/

All other pictures – http://www.howtocreateafamilymuseum.blogspot.com

Graduations

Graduation Cap – https://www.google.com/search

Scene from Othello – https://beau-english.wikispaces.com

All High School Pictures – http://www.howtocreateafamilymuseum.blogspot.com

How to Organize Your Heirlooms: Find, Select, Display

Teamwork – https://images.google.com

Career pictures – http://www.howtocreateafamilymuseum.blogspot.com

All drawings – http://www.howtocreateafamilymuseum.blogspot.com

Art Framing – http://www.michaels.com/display-cases-and-shadowboxes/kids-art/840874383

School box – http://www.howtocreateafamilymuseum.blogspot.com

Art storage – http://www.displays4sale.com/StoreModules/ProductDetails.aspx?p=Plastic-Swinging-Panel-Poster-Displays

Where to Begin – 5 Steps

Box of stuff - http://charity.lovetoknow.com/Donate_Used_Toys

Make a list - http://bluelabelhost.com

Think - https://angelahovan.files.wordpress.com/2015/02/guessing.jpg?w=240

Art of Display

Antique Store display - http://www.antiquevillageva.com

Dormer Window – https://www.google.com/search?biw=1727&bih=838&tbm=isch&sa=1&q=
children+bedroom+dormer+windows&oq=children+bedroom+dormer+windows

Illustration Credits for Images

Curio cabinet – https://images.google.com

Picture, dolls, dresser – http://www.howtocreateafamilymuseum.blogspot.com

Curio cabinet – https://www.subastralinc.com/square-display-case-with-light.html

Hanging rug – http://carpet.vidalondon.net/used-carpets/

Be a Curator – Part I

Plastic storage bin – http://www.howtocreateafamilymuseum.blogspot.com

Be a Curator – Part II

Pyramid - https://www.google.com/search?q=pyramids

Rolling storage rack – https://www.pinterest.com/beetooo/drift-ideas/

Every child Artist poster – https://www.etsy.com/market/kids_art_display

Shadowbox with seashells – http://www.inhabitots.com

Household Inventory book – http://www.howtocreateafamilymuseum.blogspot.com

Antique photo album – https://images.google.com/

Old Photographs – http://www.wisegeek.com/how-do-i-preserve-photos.htm

Photo Album - http://www.galleryleather.com/photo-albums/travel-window

Computer discs – http://www.publicdomainpictures.net/view-image.php?image=491

Interviewing Family – https://www.nps.gov/parkhistory/oralhistory.htm

Movie camera – http://www.lizardfish.co.uk/#!Kodak-Super-8-Camera

Old Letters – http://www.howtocreateafamilymuseum.blogspot.com

Old typewriter – http://www.gettyimages.com/detail/photo/old-vintage-typewriter

Archives folders – http://www.gloucestercitynews.net/clearysnotebook

How to Build a Family Museum – Building Materials

Building Tools – http://deideiabuja.wixsite.com/deidei

Select Hardwoods – http://www.greatspirithardwoods.com/machinery-woodworking.php

Solid hardwoods – http://solidflooringpaloalto.com/hardwood-flooring/

Melamine Laminates – http://kunrunwoodzxy.en.ec21.com

More samples of wood veneers – https://www.pinterest.com/explore/wood-stain-colors/

Shelf hardware – http://www.decoware.info

Glass Shelves – https://images.google.com

Illustration Credits for Images

Glass Shelf bookcase – https://images.google.com

Glass Seamed Edge – http://www.glassprocessing.com.au/products_float_glass.html

Spot lights – http://www.lowes.com

Gallery Lights – https://images.google.com

Rope Lights – http://www.noveltylights.com/clear-rope-lights-custom-cut

Museum Curtains - http://www.howtocreateafamilymuseum.blogspot.com

Heirloom display – https://images.google.com

Where to Locate – Living Room

Coffee Table - http://www.home-museum.com/hobbies/Antiques/antiques.html

Coffee Table - https://www.pinterest.com/shannoncarmi/amber/

Coffee Table - http://jgcustomartdisplay.com/tables.html

Mollica Figurines & Piano - http://www.howtocreateafamilymuseum.blogspot.com

Where to Locate – Dining Room

Nippon Vases – http://www.howtocreateafamilymuseum.blogspot.com

Nippon Mark – https://www.kovels.com/price-guide/pottery-porcelain-price-guide/nippon.html

Dining Room Suite, china & compote – http://www.howtocreateafamilymuseum.blogspot.com

Where to Locate – Family Room

Family Room - http://cdn.cnsnews.com/images/ap%20tv%20set.jpg

Rumpus Room - http://www.vowles-au.com/images/jpg/Rumpus%20Room5.jpg

White bookcase with fireplace - http://lisa-notlaksa.blogspot.com/2012/10/media-room-speakers.html

White bookcase with big screen TV - http://shelter.typepad.com

Wood bookcase with big screen TV - http://www.houzz.com

Coffee Table - http://www.designsofthewest.com/displaycoffee.html

Where to Locate – Hallways/Ledges

Ledges - https://www.pinterest.com/pin/550565123166244102/

Modern ledges - https://www.amazon.com/Burnes-Boston-LL2931-Level-Walnut/dp/B000B4X8UY

Gallery light - https://www.lightingdirect.com

Where to Locate – Hallways/Shadow Boxes

Gloves in shadowbox - http://wistariahurst.org

Illustration Credits for Images

Jewelry in shadowbox - http://www.carteravenueframeshop.com

Mask in Shadow box - http://www.howtocreateafamilymuseum.blogspot.com

Lizzie's jewelry in shadowbox - http://www.howtocreateafamilymuseum.blogspot.com

Guitars in shadowbox – http://www.home-museum.com

Teddy Bear in shadowbox – http://www.home-museum.com

Military shadowbox - http://cheapmilitarysurplusclothing.blogspot.com

Army pins in shadowbox – http://artimagesfrom.com/military-shadow-boxes/oramasnautical.com

Where to Locate – Master Bedroom

All pictures – http://www.howtocreateafamilymuseum.blogspot.com

Where to Locate – Child(s) Bedroom

Pink Bedroom – http://www.kampur.com

Bedroom with Cabinets – http://www.zillow.com/digs/contemporary-kids-bedrooms-5359854518/

Charlie's Bedroom – http://www.howtocreateafamilymuseum.blogspot.com

Dormer space – https://images.google.com

Dormer Window – https://www.google.com/search?biw=1727&bih=838&tbm=isch&sa=1&q=children+bedroom+dormer+windows&oq=children+bedroom+dormer+windows

Where to Locate – Guestroom

Modern Curio Cabinet – http://www.showplacerents.com/browse?pid=929727323

Art Deco Cabinet – http://www.antiquehelper.com/catalog-search?q=deco&page=65&sort=

Museum Gel – https://www.amazon.com/Ready-America-33111-Museum-Clear/dp/B0002V37XY

Traditional Cabinet – http://www.houzz.com

Shaker Cabinet – http://www.amishoutletstore.com

Where to Locate – Home Office

Home Office – http://www.homeviewers.xyz/home-office-decorating-ideas/

All Home Office pictures – http://www.howtocreateafamilymuseum.blogspot.com

Where to Locate – Office away from Home

Office away from home – http://display-smart.com/blog/page/4/

Office display cabinet – http://display-smart.com

Trophy Cabinet – http://display-smart.com

Illustration Credits for Images

Where to Locate – Closets and Shelving

Closet Units – http://www.houzz.com

Messy closet - http://www.howtocreateafamilymuseum.blogspot.com

Clean closet – https://images.google.com

Closet – http://second-sun.co/master-bathroom-closet-combo/master-closet-with-window-remodel/

Doors to Museum – http://www.howtocreateafamilymuseum.blogspot.com

Inside a closet – http://www.houzz.com/photos/1538847/Closet-Systems-traditional-closet-birmingham

Closet rendering – https://images.google.com

Museum Sign – http://www.howtocreateafamilymuseum.blogspot.com

Where to Locate – Any Room - Custom-Built Units

Custom Bookshelf – http://www.diyadvice.com/diy/built-ins/storage/cabinets-with-cushions/

Keith & Lizzie's Museum – http://www.howtocreateafamilymuseum.blogspot.com

Modular Bookcase – https://yubecube.com/

Interior Wall shelf – http://samsonscarpentry.weebly.com/cabinets--shelving--millwork.html

White Shelves – https://www.pinterest.com/pin/308355905707640780/

Hall Display case – http://hative.com/ikea-billy-hacks/

Stairway shelves – http://www.houzz.com

Under the stairway shelves – https://www.pinterest.com/milenamornelas/decor-embaixo-de-escadas/

Over the door shelf - http://www.houzz.com/display-shelf-above-door

Around the window shelves - http://foter.com/explore/window-benches

Styrofoam Blocks – http://www.michaels.com/10302810.html#start=24

Wood blocks – https://www.amazon.com/Woodpeckers

Step-shelves – http://www.candyconceptsinc.com/Counter-Wooden-Stair-Step-Display_p_4681.html

Museum step-shelves – http://www.howtocreateafamilymuseum.blogspot.com

Acrylic step-shelves – https://www.alibaba.com

Glass display case – http://www.westelm.com

Glass box – http://www.westelm.com/products/glass-shadow-boxes-d1399/?cm_src=PIPRecentView

Easels – http://wholesaleeasels.net/

All other pictures – http://www.howtocreateafamilymuseum.blogspot.com

Illustration Credits for Images

The Single Life

Two Curio Cabinets - https://www.subastralinc.com/display-cases/wall-display-cases.html?limit=all

Craftsmen Curio – http://hawaiiforest.org/woodshow/woodshow93.html

Granma's Curio – https://www.pinterest.com/cooks927/curio-cabinet-redo/

Curio Display – https://www.wayfair.com/

Museum Gel – https://www.amazon.com/Ready-America-33111-Museum-Clear/dp/B0002V37XY

Think Out of the Box

Mausoleum – http://www.howtocreateafamilymuseum.blogspot.com

Storefront – http://www.maplewoodvillagemhp.com/shopping.html

Storage units – http://www.eastlongmeadowstorage.com/spaceestimator/

Tiny House – https://mdesigninteriors.files.wordpress.com/2012/08/harbinger-310sf.jpg

Objective of Organization

Magnifying glass – http://clipart-library.com/data_images/141546.jpg

All Renderings – http://www.howtocreateafamilymuseum.blogspot.com

Old photos – http://www.wisegeek.org/what-is-the-best-way-to-store-photos.htm#old-photographs

All Memory Boxes – http://www.howtocreateafamilymuseum.blogspot.com

Stack of papers – http://www.clipartkid.com/stack-of-paper-icon-clipart-panda-free-clipart-images-TXhKpk-clipart/

Last Will – https://images.google.com

Maintenance - Conservation and Preservation, Cataloging and Storage

Conservatory chest – http://www.home-museum.com/products/prod-top-level/prod-top.html

File cabinets – http://woodcarte.com/showroom/home-office/file-cabinets/

Map chest – http://www.home-museum.com/products/prod-top-level/prod-top.html

Preservations boxes – http://www.dickblick.com/products/blick-archival-storage-boxes/

Preserving your Papers

Judges hammer – http://f.tqn.com/y/divorcesupport/1/L/1/4/-/-/SO001547.jpg

Military Discharge papers – https://www.google.com/search?q=military+discharge+papers&source

Archival storage – http://www.dickblick.com/products/blick-archival-storage-boxes/

Illustration Credits for Images

Introduction to Our Family Museums

Museum sign — http://www.howtocreateafamilymuseum.blogspot.com

The Parents Museum

Parents Museum – http://www.howtocreateafamilymuseum.blogspot.com

Our Baby Toys

All toys – http://www.howtocreateafamilymuseum.blogspot.com

Keith's vintage horse toy – https://www.worthpoint.com/worthopedia/steven-rock-a-toy-balancing-toy

Liz's Baby vintage dish – https://www.pinterest.com/pin/133208101451922881/

All other pictures – http://www.howtocreateafamilymuseum.blogspot.com

Liz's Kitchen set – https://picclick.com/Vintage-Wolverine-Toy-Sink-Dishwasher-Tin-Lithograph-1950s-391442959759.html

Childhood Clothes

All clothes – http://www.howtocreateafamilymuseum.blogspot.com

Catalog page – https://envisioningtheamericandream.com/2012/12/23/mail-order-madnessgifts-and-guns-galore/catalog-guns-dresses/

Vintage Baby Books

Blue & Yellow Baby Books – http://www.howtocreateafamilymuseum.blogspot.com

Keith's Awana Club

All Awana pictures – http://www.howtocreateafamilymuseum.blogspot.com

Keith's Baseball Memories

2014 World Series – https://en.wikipedia.org/wiki/2014_World_Series

White Sox logo – http://www.sportslogos.net/logos/list_by_team/55/Chicago_White_Sox/

NY Mets picture – https://en.wikipedia.org/wiki/New_York_Metropolitans

All Baseball pictures – http://www.howtocreateafamilymuseum.blogspot.com

Cracker Jack box – https://en.wikipedia.org/wiki/Cracker_Jack

Ted Williams – http://www.baseball-reference.com/players/w/willite01.shtml

Vintage School Books

All school books – http://www.howtocreateafamilymuseum.blogspot.com

Illustration Credits for Images

Our Wedding

All Wedding pictures – http://www.howtocreateafamilymuseum.blogspot.com

Gown label – http://vintagefashionguild.org/label-resource/priscilla-of-boston/

A gown in shadow box – http://vatly.info/20160911105702_wedding-dress-display-frame/

Leisure Suits & Hot Pants

Illustration of men's leisure suits – https://www.pinterest.com/perrymorse/men-s-vintage-clothing-patterns/

Peach suit & Hot pants – http://www.howtocreateafamilymuseum.blogspot.com

Stewardess in hot pants – https://www.pinterest.com/pin/54887689178827322/

Twiggy in hot pants – https://www.pinterest.com/sitechic/twiggy-3/

Liz in hot pants pictures – http://www.howtocreateafamilymuseum.blogspot.com

Eye Glasses

All frames & case – http://www.howtocreateafamilymuseum.blogspot.com

Illustration of face shapes – http://www.allaboutvision.com/eyeglasses/eyeglasses_shape_color_analysis.htm

Cat Eye frames - https://www.pinterest.com/pin/222506037820286135/

Vintage Makeup Collection

All Makeup pictures – http://www.howtocreateafamilymuseum.blogspot.com

Keep Calm sign – https://www.pinterest.com/pin/469781804852846074/

Vintage Shoes

All shoe pictures – http://www.howtocreateafamilymuseum.blogspot.com

Toy and Keepsake

Keith's Doll – http://www.howtocreateafamilymuseum.blogspot.com

Herbert Bank – https://picclick.com/Vintage-HARRIS-LION-BANK-HUBERT-CERAMIC-WITH-GLASSES-282354565616.html

Hubert Lion - https://www.youtube.com/watch?v=5jbd-7dvd1w

The Children's Museum

Picture of children's museum - http://www.howtocreateafamilymuseum.blogspot.com

All toy pictures - http://www.howtocreateafamilymuseum.blogspot.com

Their Christening Kegs

All pictures - http://www.howtocreateafamilymuseum.blogspot.com

Illustration Credits for Images

Baby Clothes and Toys

All photos - http://www.howtocreateafamilymuseum.blogspot.com

Play Mobil dollhouse - https://www.pinterest.com/pin/531565562241301914/

Charlie's Side

All toy photos - http://www.howtocreateafamilymuseum.blogspot.com

Toys for Tots logo - http://m.toysfortots.org/mobile/default.html?4

Thomas the Tank - https://en.wikipedia.org/wiki/Thomas_the_Tank_Engine

Charlie's Nickel Collection

Storage drawers – http://www.home-museum.com/hobbies/Coins/coins.html

Box of nickels – https://www.cointalk.com/threads/6-boxes-of-nickels.290551/

Buffalo head nickel – http://www.garfieldrefining.com/history-of-american-buffalo-coin

Stack of nickels – http://www.goldwhy.com/gold-images/stacks-of-us-silver-coins.jpg

Tiffeni's Side

All photos - http://www.howtocreateafamilymuseum.blogspot.com

Tiffeni' Eclectic Collections

All pictures - http://www.howtocreateafamilymuseum.blogspot.com

Introduction to the Grandparent's Museum

All pictures - http://www.howtocreateafamilymuseum.blogspot.com

Step-by-Step Assembly Guide

All pictures - http://www.howtocreateafamilymuseum.blogspot.com

Maternal and Paternal Grandparent's Museum

All pictures – http://www.howtocreateafamilymuseum.blogspot.com

Dad's Story

All pictures – http://www.howtocreateafamilymuseum.blogspot.com

My Mother's Story

All pictures – http://www.howtocreateafamilymuseum.blogspot.com

Trianon Ballroom postcard - http://chicagopatterns.com/trianon-worlds-most-beautiful-ballroom/

Aragon Ballroom postcard - http://www.encyclopedia.chicagohistory.org/pages/58.html

Illustration Credits for Images

Maternal and Paternal Grandparent's Museum

Picture of Sami People - https://en.wikipedia.org/wiki/Sami_people

All pictures – http://www.howtocreateafamilymuseum.blogspot.com

Grandparents Museum/ Great Aunt Gitta's Doll

Picture of doll & cradle - http://www.howtocreateafamilymuseum.blogspot.com

Grandparents Museum/ Aunt Alice – Missionary

All pictures - http://www.howtocreateafamilymuseum.blogspot.com

The Grandchildren's Museum on Their Father's Side

All pictures - http://www.howtocreateafamilymuseum.blogspot.com

The Next Generation

All pictures - http://www.howtocreateafamilymuseum.blogspot.com

Illustration Credits for Images

The links for these resources were available at the time of publication.

About the Author

Elizabeth Goesel, former Fine Arts dealer and art gallery proprietor, Docent at a Fine Arts Museum, published author on 18th Century Colonial American history, enthusiastic collector and eager genealogist and avid memorialist, enjoys writing recollections, appreciates the efforts of conservators, archeologists, even treasure hunters in their quest to preserve, maintain and display worldly as well as unassuming things. Then one day, decided to do the same and created a Family Museum. After the museums were created: The Parent's Museum; The Children's Museum; The Grandparent's Museum, a Blog was written detailing the steps taken on how to create a Family Museum with this purpose in mind:

From childhood to young adult, schools, careers, travels, relationships, marriage, parenthood and retirement, my family and I moved from place to place, accumulated, inherited and bought stuff. Many boxes filled up, were moved around, some got lost, some got trashed, and some were kept. Within all of this boxed and bagged stuff, there were some truly worthy keepsakes.

Then she asked herself what should she do with all this stuff? The answer came to her from an unexpected source that inspired her to create a Family Museum.

Though there was a lot of work cleaning out attics, basements, storage units, and going through tons of boxes, many phenomenal treasures were found. Some with monetary value, most without except for the priceless, precious, inestimable, and most importantly, irreplaceable objects from her family's past.

Once the unthinkable and improbable Family Museum was completed (but never finished, like history itself), she decided to write a blog to enlighten, share and inspire families, individuals, even businesses, to create a personal museum. Post-by-post, she describe how to achieve this wonderful endeavor.

After four years of posts, this book was published and made available to all those who seek a way to honor their ancestors by displaying and protecting their history to pass down to the next generation. Her Blog will continue to post stories, supported by informative writings to offer inspiration.

Her blogs address is: http://howtocreateafamilymuseum.blogspot.com and she can found on Facebook and Twitter.

Acknowledgements

This endeavor is dedicated to my Family: Husband, Keith; Daughter, Tiffeni; and Son, Charlie. Without them our Family Museum would not be what it is today.

From the beginning, Keith constructed the museum, fashioning what would have been a linen closet into a closet full of history. With his expert carpentry skills, he measured, cut, and nailed the shelves into place. He painted the walls and hung beautiful French Doors, enhanced by hand-crafted molding. Then he designed and hung an entertaining sign letting everyone who passed by that this was our Family Museum.

Tiffeni is a historian at heart. She started collecting antiques at an early age. She treasured all the stories told to her by her grandparents, played in the attic where she found many of the treasurers that are in our museum today. She as the memory of an elephant, able to recall where and when she had the toy, book, outfit, picture, you name it. Many times I would have to ask her where something came from and from whom. She would help me with researching, with displaying, and she even drew up our first Family Tree. She is indispensable and I know she will guard our Family history with steadfast care.

Charlie loves to tell stories. Not through the written word, but the spoken one, captivating the listener with his antics and vivid descriptions. He wants to keep everything and tell you all about it, and charms all who become entranced with his storytelling. He is always contributing things to the museum, challenging me to find space for it. He, too, as an historian's heart and his passion for maritime history is overwhelming with his ship models, books and keepsakes. He has accumulated, saved and cherishes his collections so much that he could create a museum of his own. Like his sister, he too will guard and protect the family heirlooms and pass them on to the next generation.

I am profoundly thankful to my father, Bill, for if it wasn't his tenacity to save just about everything that he could, I would not have what I do today. He told me time and time again, "Lisbit, never throw anything away because you never know when you might need it." I truly didn't think I would need to keep my old toys, books, school papers, even old love letters. But my dad did this for me and when I found these things from my past, they became today's treasures. And when I found – actually Tiffeni found them first – his writings about his life, from young manhood to a Navy man, married man and father, to a business man, builder and keeper of the family heirlooms, our museum would not exist today. Thank you, Dad,

Before Keith's mom, Gladys passed away, she made sure that rather than have her children quibble over who gets what, she made everyone put their name on whatever they wanted to have before she was no longer with us. This future-looking lady was very smart, indeed, and knew how best to handle what normally could turn out to be a tenuous situation. And as we selected what we wanted, she graciously told us the story behind the item, endowing us with much family history, and it is this history that is now safely displayed and cared for in our Grandparents Museum. Gladys was also the inspiration for other family members and when her sister passed away, we received other family heirlooms and the stories that went with them.

A special Thank You to Leslie Wolfinger, Publishing Director for Heritage Books, who believes in this endeavor to promote saving family heritage, and Debbie Riley, Editor, for her diligence and patience. And a heartfelt thankyou to my friends who were impressed with the concept and encouraged me to carry on. And I sincerely hope this book will motivate all to create their Family Museum.

0116

CPSIA information can be obtained
at www.ICGtesting.com
Printed in the USA
LVHW101925050820
662460LV00003B/258